Tampa Bay through the *Times*

St. Petersburg Times

Acknowledgments

Work for this project actually began decades before it was conceived. The *St. Petersburg Times* would like to thank the photographers, reporters, editors and newsmakers who have been a part of our coverage from the late 1800s through today. Without them, this book would have been an impossibility.

We also would like to thank the people who have called this slice of the west coast of Florida home. We are especially indebted to the early settlers whose lives were captured in photographs that allow us a glimpse into what the days were like 125 years ago – and to the people who thought it important to preserve those images.

We received generous help from the archives of the following organizations: the Tampa-Hillsborough County Public Library System, the Nelson Poynter Memorial Library at the University of South Florida St. Petersburg, Pinellas County's Heritage Village Archives & Library and the St. Petersburg Museum of History. David Shedden, director of the library at the Poynter Institute for Media Studies, was another great resource.

Our thanks go to employees of the *Times* who worked on this project: Claire Giglio, Carolyn V. Alderson, Amanda DeArmon, James McCarthy, Christopher Sturgeon and Vicki Zook of the Archives department; Mary Mellstrom and John Martin of News Research; Richard Proplesch of Photo; Barbara Moch and Chris Miller of Copy Services; Andi Gordon of Advertising; Jerry Hill, Robin Lankton, Paul Coffey, Jill Kalber, Rick Flannigan and Susan Halttunen of Audience Development; Teresa Hyre of Finance; and executive news editor John Schlander.

We also wish to give special recognition to two *Times* editors who spent a few weeks researching cutline information, gathering and scanning photos and writing and editing much of this book. Deputy managing editor Rob Hooker, who wrote introductions to each chapter, has a master's degree in history from Vanderbilt University. He was the editor and writer of a special section devoted to the *Times'* 100th anniversary in 1984. Newsart director Ron Brackett, who is also a history buff, was editor of a special report on the 50th anniversary of the Korean War and a special section devoted to the 60th anniversary of the end of World War II. Their many contributions made this book possible.

Finally, we wish to acknowledge the historians and journalists whose earlier work helped inform the material presented here. The historians include Raymond Arsenault and Gary R. Mormino of the University of South Florida St. Petersburg, St. Petersburg Mayor Rick Baker, Anthony P. Pizzo and Hampton Dunn of Tampa, Michael L. Sanders of Clearwater and Karl H. Grismer, Walter P. Fuller and Enoch Davis of St. Petersburg. The *Times* journalists include Jon Wilson, Tom C. Harris, Dick Bothwell, Mary Jo Melone, Teresa Burney, Dan DeWitt and Bob Jensen.

Members of the St. Petersburg Times
125th Anniversary Committee

Ron Brackett
Pauline Brockman
Rick Flannigan
Gerald Gifford
Anne Glover
Andi Gordon
Craig Holley
Jill Kalber
Robin Lankton
Alvin Nesmith
Christine Paul
Jane Peppard
David Shedden
Ericka Watson

Published by Pediment Publishing, a division of The Pediment Group, Inc. www.pediment.com Printed in Canada

Contents

Foreword

Some people come to Florida for a good time. The pages that follow hold photos of Joe DiMaggio, Marilyn Monroe and Elvis Presley. When Babe Ruth was in St. Petersburg for spring training, he observed: "If anyone can have fun in this town, I can."

And some people come to Florida for good. Over the years, the west coast of Florida has been transformed by people who decided this wasn't just a good place to visit, but that they wanted to live here.

Among those people who saw this region's potential was a family named Poynter. They came here from southern Indiana, and purchased the local newspaper, the *St. Peters-burg Times*. Their son Nelson raised the *Times'* standards and its sights, and he launched it on a path toward state and national prominence.

He did something else remarkable. Before he died 30 years ago, Poynter created a school dedicated to journalism training, and he left the newspaper to it. He wanted to make sure the newspaper remained independent, locally owned and an asset to its community. Every town deserves a newspaper that loves it best, Poynter liked to say.

This book is a partial record of the relationship between the newspaper and the town. In their origins, neither one amounted to much.

Way back when, baseball fans gathered around the newspaper offices, while the editors called out the running score of World Series games from the telegraph wire. They could not have imagined that their town would have its own baseball team playing for its own spot in the World Series, or that the newspaper could send that news around the world on something called the Internet.

As the town grew, so did the newspaper. It campaigned to protect the waterfront from development. It fought to carve out a separate county for the peninsula, and as the area grew, it tried to knit the pieces back together again into a larger community of Tampa Bay. It celebrated the triumphs, like the birth of a new university, and it mourned the tragedies, like the collapse of the Sunshine Skyway bridge.

As time went by, as their owners died or lost interest, most newspapers around America were collected into chains, usually with corporate headquarters far from the cities where they are published. But because of Nelson Poynter's remarkable decision, the *Times* is still rooted here in Tampa Bay.

Sometimes readers take delight in the *Times*; occasionally they are stirred to outrage. But they never have to wonder where its loyalties lie. In many ways, the *Times* has thrived because our region has, too. In turn, the newspaper has endeavored to be an asset and an advocate for the community. The town is older, bigger and more complex, but it still has a newspaper that loves it best.

This is an important birthday for the *Times*, and this album is one way of celebrating with the neighbors who helped us reach that milestone. I like to think that far into the future, new generations will turn to the *Times* – in one form or another – as history unfolds in Tampa Bay.

Perhaps one day they will look back on images from this, our own modern era, and marvel: "how quaint."

Paul Tash
Editor & Chairman

LEFT: Nelson Poynter, seen in the portrait on the easel, helped ensure the *St. Petersburg Times* would remain locally owned by handpicking his successor, a practice followed by subsequent leaders of the *Times*. From left, Eugene Patterson, CEO from 1978 to 1988, Paul Tash, 2004 to present, and Andy Barnes, 1988 to 2004, at the Poynter Institute for Media Studies in St. Petersburg.

The Late 1800s

Although statehood came to Florida in 1845, west-central Florida did not come alive for another 40 years. It took the pluck of some pioneering farmers and fishermen, the money of a handful of daring entrepreneurs and – more than anything – the arrival of the iron horse. The railroad gave life to the small, sleepy town of Tampa and a number of hamlets scattered along the Gulf Coast.

For much of the 19th century, most of the region was still raw frontier. A monster hurricane in 1848 swamped most of the Pinellas peninsula in a huge storm surge and all but wiped out Fort Brooke, a military outpost established in 1824 in what is now downtown Tampa. Then came the Civil War, Reconstruction and some financial missteps by the state, which left state government staggering under a mountain of bonded indebtedness. Emancipation from the yoke of debt came in 1881, when Hamilton Disston, a Philadelphia tool manufacturer, bought 4-million acres from the state. The cash helped the state settle its debt and ushered in a modest land boom and spate of railroad construction.

As the 1880s began, Tampa (which may have gotten its name from a 16th century Indian village) had a population of 720. Then transportation tycoon Henry B. Plant decided to bring his railroad from Kissimmee to Tampa. In just seven years, he also helped lure cigar manufacturers away from Key West, founded Port Tampa and built a palatial hotel (now the University of Tampa).

The peninsula across the bay got its name from early Spanish explorers, who dubbed it Punta Pinal, or point of the pines. In the mid 1880s, the only settlements of consequence were Clear Water Harbor and Dunedin (the Gaelic word for Edinburgh, the Scottish home of early settlers). Combined, their population was about 300. That began to change when an aristocratic Russian immigrant named Pyotr Alexeyevitch Dementyev took over the Orange Belt Railroad in central Florida. In 1888, Peter Demens – as he called himself in America – brought the railroad through Pasco County to Clear Water and then south to a ramshackle settlement that got the name St. Petersburg in honor of Demens' home in Russia.

As Pinellas grew, a humble newspaper was there to chronicle developments. *The West Hillsborough Times*, a four-page weekly in Dunedin, began publishing July 25, 1884. The men who founded it – a physician, a dentist and a printer – sold it four months later to Arthur C. Turner, a merchant who moved it 5 miles south to Clear Water Harbor. In 1892, the paper was sold again and moved to St. Petersburg.

LEFT: View of the main street in St. Petersburg looking out on the bay, 1890s. In the early years the streets were often impassable, clogged with dust and loose sand in dry weather, under water in wet. It took several half-hearted attempts and a pair of ordinances, plus money in the public coffers, for the town to finally begin improving its streets. *Courtesy Archives of the St. Petersburg Times*

Salutatory, December 4, 1884

"We greet the readers of the *Times* as kindly as this style of introduction will permit – gladly observing that they have already become a numerous family, and fondly trusting that their numbers will soon increase a hundred fold.... We expect, and shall try very hard, to tell the truth; but it will take a long time to tell the whole truth about even this small territory which we especially represent."

ABOVE: The first hotel in the newly named community of St. Petersburg is the Detroit at Central Avenue and Second Street, circa 1888. It is named to honor the hometown of John Constantine Williams, one of St. Petersburg's founders.
Courtesy St. Petersburg Museum of History

TOP RIGHT: Tom Beanblossom (holding the knife) is the proud hunter who killed this eight-point deer in 1886. The photo was taken at the home of Arthur C. Turner, a Clear Water Harbor (now Clearwater) merchant who owned the *Times* from December 1884 to the fall of 1892. *Courtesy Heritage Village Archives & Library*

BOTTOM RIGHT PHOTOS: The *West Hillsborough Times* begins publication July 25, 1884, as a four-page weekly in Dunedin. Its principal financier is J.L. Edgar, left, a physician; its editor, J.M. "Doc" Baggett, center, a dentist; its printer, M. Joel McMullen, right. The type is set by hand, one letter at a time, and two of the pages are preprinted in Atlanta. Four months later, the paper is sold and moved to Clear Water Harbor.

Our Railroad
Prospects, December 16, 1886

"We regard the prospect for a railroad into our midst during the year 1887, as being most encouraging. The fact that the managers of the Orange Belt R.R. are now in our section, manifesting considerable interest in regard to our railroad affairs, assures us that we are worthy of some degree of interest."

LEFT: Orange Belt Railway Station, Clear Water Harbor (now Clearwater), 1888. *Courtesy Heritage Village Archives & Library*

BELOW: Orange Belt Railway Locomotive #10, circa 1895. When the first train chugged into a tiny community in the southern part of the peninsula on June 8, 1888, it marked the birth of St. Petersburg, so named because one of the city's founders was from St. Petersburg, Russia. *Courtesy St. Petersburg Museum of History*

ABOVE: In 1890 the Paxton House becomes St. Petersburg's second hotel. It offers 32 rooms at the northwest corner of Central Avenue and First Street. *Courtesy Archives of the St. Petersburg Times*

TOP: Richard J. Morgan, shown with a Simplex press, buys the *West Hillsborough Times* for $1,200 and moves it from Clear Water Harbor to St. Petersburg. As the new editor, Morgan experiments with different names: the *Times*, the *News*, the *Once a Week*, but by 1894 or 1895, he settles on the *St. Petersburg Times* as the new name. *Courtesy Archives of the St. Petersburg Times*

TOP LEFT: An interior view of Exchange National Bank in 1894, Tampa. *Courtesy Tampa-Hillsborough County Public Library System*

LEFT: One of the first people to come to St. Petersburg was John Donaldson, a former slave who arrived in 1868 and bought 40 acres three years later. The first bloc of black settlers were workmen who helped build the railroad into St. Petersburg in 1888. *Courtesy Heritage Village Archives & Library*

OPPOSITE: Passengers seated in the Tampa Suburban Co. double-decker streetcar on Ballast Point Route in Tampa, 1892. *Courtesy Tampa-Hillsborough County Public Library System*

ABOVE: Conductor Billie Hill and brakeman Robert Pepper of the Gulf Coast Express on Orange Belt line, St. Petersburg, 1895. *Courtesy Heritage Village Archives & Library*

TOP RIGHT: Turner and Wilson Coffee Roasters delivery wagon, Tampa, 1895 *Courtesy Tampa-Hillsborough County Public Library System*

RIGHT: Clear Water Harbor city pier, at the foot of Cleveland Street, 1890s. *Courtesy Heritage Village Archives & Library*

OPPOSITE: Cigar manufacturers play cards at the Cherokee Club in Tampa, 1895. In the late 1800s thousands of immigrants from Spain, Cuba and Italy came to Tampa's Ybor City to make cigars by hand. *Courtesy Tampa-Hillsborough County Public Library System*

ABOVE: Craig Can Meter, left, and A.R. Elliott on the railroad tracks in front of the Ozona station, circa 1895.
Courtesy Heritage Village Archives & Library

TOP RIGHT: Interior of Bradshaw's drugstore on the northeast corner of Central Avenue and Second Street in St. Petersburg, circa 1896. The owner of this store, James G. Bradshaw, later served as mayor from 1913 to 1916. From left are Mr. Stolley, clerk; Mr. Ross, Bradshaw and Dr. Claude Prannon. *Courtesy St. Petersburg Museum of History*

RIGHT: Belleview Biltmore Hotel under construction in 1896 in what is now Belleair. The hotel, still receiving guests today, opened on January 15, 1897. *Courtesy Tampa-Hillsborough County Public Library System*

ABOVE: Theodore Roosevelt poses with spearfishing guide Russell J. Colio at Boca Ciega Bay, St. Petersburg. Years earlier, in 1898, Roosevelt's Rough Riders spent time in Tampa before embarking to fight in Cuba during the Spanish-American War.
Courtesy Tampa-Hillsborough County Public Library System

TOP LEFT: Henry Plant supervised the transport of Army troops by railroad to Port Tampa, where they boarded ships to fight the Spanish-American War in Cuba, 1898. *Courtesy Archives of the St. Petersburg Times*

BOTTOM LEFT: The Port Tampa Naval Reserve parades in 1897 on Franklin Street. The photo is looking north from Grand Central Avenue (now Kennedy Boulevard) in Tampa.
Courtesy Archives of the St. Petersburg Times

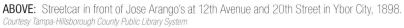

The Early 1900s

As the 20th century dawned, the communities of Tampa Bay were settling into roles that would endure for many years. St. Petersburg (population 1,575) and Clearwater (343) increasingly attracted the tourists and winter visitors who became key to their economies. In Tarpon Springs (541), the sponge industry took hold after a New York sponge buyer saw potential in the Anclote River. In 1905, several hundred Greek divers descended on the town in response to ads in their country's newspapers.

Tampa (15,839) was becoming an industrial hub with a newly deepened port, a thriving phosphate industry and scores of factories in Ybor City, where more than 100-million cigars were made by hand each year.

Societal patterns were taking hold, too. All the elected officials were white men, and so were almost all the business leaders. A middle- or upper-class white woman's place was the home, where she nurtured her husband and children. Much of the hard labor went to black men, the domestic work to black women. In housing, education, recreation and criminal justice, Jim Crow ruled.

It was a time of firsts. The event that became

Gasparilla, the annual invasion of Tampa by society leaders masquerading as pirates, came in 1904. The first benches in downtown St. Petersburg were installed in 1908 (they were orange, not green). The nation's first regularly scheduled commercial flight came in 1914, when pilot Tony Jannus flew from St. Petersburg to Tampa. That same year the St. Louis Browns held spring workouts in St. Petersburg, which became the unofficial spring training capital of Florida. Three years later, Clearwater and Clearwater Beach were linked by a bridge, but crossing the wobbly wooden structure was an adventure.

No Pinellas leader was more influential than *Times* editor W.L. Straub, who bought the paper in 1901 and became a crusader for better roads and sidewalks, strong schools, a publicly owned waterfront and independence for the Pinellas peninsula, which the Legislature split off from Hillsborough County in 1912. Straub sold the paper (now published six days a week) to Indiana publisher Paul Poynter that same year, but he remained an editorial voice for 27 years.

When the United States entered World War I, hundreds of men from the bay area answered Uncle Sam's call. A ship that bore Tampa's name, the Coast Guard cutter USS *Tampa*, was sunk by a German U-boat in September 1918. Aboard were 23 men from Tampa and at least two from St. Petersburg. All perished.

LEFT: World War I draftees from District #1 at the 400 block of Lafayette and Franklin streets in Tampa, 1917.
Courtesy Tampa-Hillsborough County Public Library System

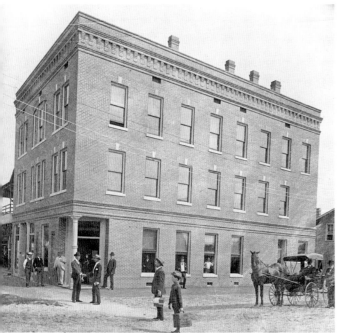

ABOVE: St. Petersburg Novelty Works at the corner of First Avenue S and Seventh Street, circa 1900. The store was owned by Abram C. Pheil, who was mayor in 1912-1913. *Courtesy St. Petersburg Historical Society*

TOP LEFT: Anclote Key Lighthouse off the coast of Tarpon Springs. It was built in 1887. *Courtesy Heritage Village Archives & Library*

LEFT: One classic column at the corner front door was featured on the First National Bank building at the corner of Central Avenue and Second Street in St. Petersburg in the early 1900s photo. To the left of the bank is Eagle Inn. *Courtesy Archives of the St. Petersburg Times*

BELOW: A view down Sixth Avenue (now Central Avenue) in St. Petersburg, looking west from the bay, circa 1900. *Courtesy Heritage Village Archives & Library*

ABOVE: Hauling grapefruit to packing house, Sutherland (now Palm Harbor), early 1900s.
Courtesy Heritage Village Archives & Library

TOP: Spraying new orange trees in Tarpon Springs, circa 1900. *Courtesy Heritage Village Archives & Library*

LEFT: S.S. Coachman & Son Groceries delivery truck, Cleveland Street near the railroad tracks, Clear Water, circa 1900. *Courtesy Heritage Village Archives & Library*

RIGHT: A fine catch on the docks in St. Petersburg, circa 1901. The man second from the right is identified as taxidermist Allie J. Thayer. *Courtesy Heritage Village Archives & Library*

BELOW: Van Gorder family members display their catch in St. Petersburg, 1900. *Courtesy Heritage Village Archives & Library*

ABOVE: Sea turtle catch on the beach in St. Petersburg, circa 1900. *Courtesy Heritage Village Archives & Library*

TOP LEFT: Boat building was a small but significant local industry in Pinellas County before World War I, early 1900s.
Courtesy Archives of the St. Petersburg Times

BOTTOM LEFT: View looking north toward the Hillsborough River from a Tampa Electric Co. smokestack, with Tampa Bay to the left, and downtown to the right, 1906. *Courtesy Tampa-Hillsborough County Public Library System*

William McKinley, September 14, 1901

"**For the second time the** bullet of an assassin has been directed against a President who had conducted a successful war. William McKinley has had to pay the price demanded of Abraham Lincoln. Both men had won their way into the hearts of the people, and in each case the shot was echoed into every home in the land."

ABOVE: Central Avenue, St. Petersburg, 1903. *Courtesy Archives of the St. Petersburg Times*

RIGHT: Front page of the *St. Petersburg Times*, June 29, 1901. *Courtesy Special Collections and Archives, Nelson Poynter Memorial Library, University of South Florida St. Petersburg*

BELOW: In the early decades of St. Petersburg, no one had more impact on the development of the town than W.L. Straub (right with folded arms). He was owner and editor of the *Times* from 1901 to 1912, and remained as editor or associate editor until 1939. He led the fight to separate Pinellas from Hillsborough County, championed wide streets, orderly city planning, and preservation and beautification of the waterfront. *Courtesy Heritage Village Archives & Library*

President Roosevelt, September 21, 1901

"Theodore Roosevelt is a very young man for the presidency, and has a world wide reputation for a certain headlong impetuosity of temperament; but he is also a well-balanced man, paradoxical as that may seem."

ABOVE: 1st Company baseball team, Fort De Soto, circa 1904. *Courtesy Heritage Village Archives & Library*

TOP LEFT: First Gasparilla Parade in Tampa, with four people seated in a decorated 1903 Cadillac, circa 1904. *Courtesy Tampa-Hillsborough County Public Library System*

LEFT: Excursion steamer docked at the Railroad Pier, St. Petersburg, circa 1904. *Courtesy Heritage Village Archives & Library*

Phone Connection with County Seat, June 28, 1902

"**An event of considerable importance** to the community in general transpired this week when the Bell Telephone Company completed their line into St. Petersburg and at once opened it for service. The first day the public was offered free use of the line and not a few tried the novel experience of calling up somebody in Tampa. The benefits of this improvement will not come in great chunks to anybody, but they are nonetheless real and important. Their value will be realized more and more as the years go by…"

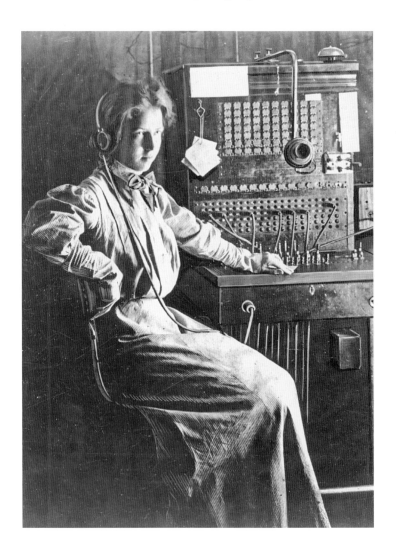

ABOVE: Elsie Hart, a telephone operator at a Peninsular Telephone Co. switchboard in 1904. *Courtesy Tampa-Hillsborough County Public Library System*

RIGHT: Front page of the *St. Petersburg Times*, December 19, 1904. *Courtesy Special Collections and Archives, Nelson Poynter Memorial Library, University of South Florida St. Petersburg*

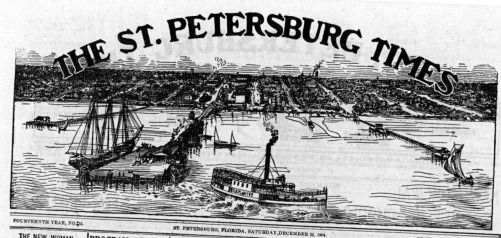

Paved Streets, July 30, 1904

"**The thing is finally fixed,** and St. Petersburg is to have brick-paved streets very soon ... The *Times* has only one suggestion to make; and that is that the first work done be a strip between the *Times* office and the post office."

ABOVE: A worker hauls crates of oranges at Eaton's Grove, west of Ninth Street near 21st Avenue N in St. Petersburg, circa 1917. *Courtesy Archives of the St. Petersburg Times*

TOP LEFT: International Bicycle Champions at the Belleview Biltmore Hotel, Belleair, circa 1905. *Courtesy Heritage Village Archives & Library*

LEFT: View of Tampa Bay from the tower, Sutherland (Palm Harbor), circa 1905. *Courtesy Heritage Village Archives & Library*

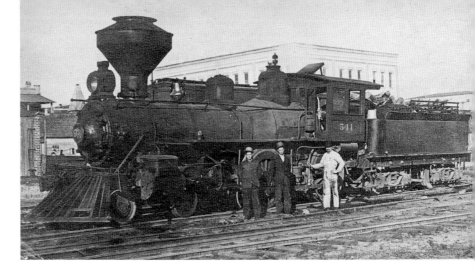

"Dealing with the Waterfront, Fall 1905

"In the *Times*' judgment – the waterfront is the most important question before the city. The bayfront is St. Petersburg's most valuable asset and it must be protected and guarded in the interest of the whole city, but the fact is it is going the other way … the waterfront should and must belong to the people …".

(W.L. Straub and the *St. Petersburg Times* campaigned for the city's acquisition of the waterfront. A few weeks before the editor's death in 1939, the City Council dedicated a section of the waterfront as Straub Park.)

ABOVE: Fishing was good in the early days, as is shown by the catches held by the men in the foreground near Hibbs Fish Co. fishhouse. It was built in 1889 and located on the Railroad Pier, which was built by the Atlantic Coast Line Railroad and extended a mile into Tampa Bay from the foot of Second Avenue S, St. Petersburg. Hibbs Fish Co. operated a fleet of boats that plied Gulf of Mexico waters as far south as the Campeche Banks on the coast of Mexico. *Courtesy Archives of the St. Petersburg Times*

TOP: Wood-burning Atlantic Coast Line Engine No. 541, St. Petersburg, 1908. *Courtesy Heritage Village Archives & Library*

ABOVE: African-Americans and Bahamians have Sunday church services at Bailey's Bluff in Pasco County, circa 1910. *Courtesy Heritage Village Archives & Library*

RIGHT: The first daily paper in St. Petersburg was the *Evening Independent,* which moved into a new building at the corner of First Avenue S and Fourth Street in 1907. For years, the *Independent* gave away the paper on any day the sun did not shine. The paper was sold to the *Times* in 1962 and folded in 1986. *Courtesy Heritage Village Archives & Library*

BOTTOM RIGHT: In 1910, fire destroys a block on the north side of Cleveland Street between Fort Harrison and Osceola avenues in Clearwater. The town then organizes its first fire department. *Courtesy Heritage Village Archives & Library*

BELOW: Charles Evans, mayor of Clearwater, laying the first brick on Cleveland Street with city engineer H.E. Anschutz and Al Frank, circa 1910. *Courtesy Heritage Village Archives & Library*

Something Different,
November 18, 1908

"No end of friends keep asking us why we don't have an automobile…we will say there is no reason in the world why we don't have a flock of automobiles except that we don't care to, besides automobiles are becoming common.

We are going to be different. We are going to have a flying machine – an aeroplane, of the Wright pattern. The *Times* force is certainly going to build one just as soon as we can possibly get around to it."

ABOVE: Hotel Poinsettia in the Roser Building, St. Petersburg, 1911. *Courtesy Heritage Village Archives & Library*

RIGHT: The Municipal Gas Plant, circa 1918. The plant opened in St. Petersburg in 1914. A large black neighborhood grew up around the plant, which later was torn down to make way for Tropicana Field. *Courtesy Archives of the St. Petersburg Times*

BELOW: The open-air post office at the corner of Fourth Street and First Avenue N, shortly after its completion in 1917. This unique Mediterranean Revival structure was designed by architect George Stewart after postmaster Roy S. Hanna secured a congressional appropriation of $107,500. *Courtesy St. Petersburg Museum of History*

February 25, 1910

"St. Petersburg schools must not be closed, so dig down into your pockets, fellow citizens, for that $2000! And as you dig you should look pleasant, for it is a glorious privilege to be owned and taxed by and for the politicians of grand old Hillsborough County."

ABOVE: St. Petersburg's first newsstand, circa 1911. Frank C. West, the owner, is shown at left with his older brother, Charles H. West. The stand was on Central Avenue between Second and Third streets. *Courtesy Archives of the St. Petersburg Times*

LEFT: Front page of the *St. Petersburg Times,* May 23, 1911. For years, the *Times* and editor Straub campaigned to have a new county, Pinellas, carved out of the western part of Hillsborough County. In 1911, the Legislature approved the separation and the governor signed it into law. A year later, a Tampa official paid tribute to Straub's role. "He (Straub) is the man behind the gun who furnished the facts and figures which took a slice off this county to make Pinellas, and if we had not fought him hard and consistently, he would have stolen Tampa Bay, the Gulf of Mexico and the furry clouds from out of our skies." *Courtesy Special Collections and Archives, Nelson Poynter Memorial Library, University of South Florida St. Petersburg*

31

ABOVE: In September 1912, Indiana newspaper publisher Paul Poynter bought the *Times* from Straub, who remained as editor. The next year Poynter (left) joined wife Alice, son Nelson, daughter Eleanor and friends on a boat outing. *Courtesy Special Collections and Archives, Nelson Poynter Memorial Library, University of South Florida St. Petersburg*

RIGHT: Front page of the *St. Petersburg Daily Times*, April 16, 1912. The editor never imagined his misspelled headline would last for a hundred years. *Courtesy Special Collections and Archives, Nelson Poynter Memorial Library, University of South Florida St. Petersburg*

BELOW: View of Sixth Avenue in Pass-A-Grille, circa 1915. A big fire destroyed this area on March 10, 1918. *Courtesy Heritage Village Archives & Library*

THE ONLY Morning Newspaper in Pinellas County

ST. PETERSBURG DAILY TIMES

ST. PETERSBURG AND PINELLAS PENINSULA HAVE THE FINEST CLIMATE IN AMERICA

Twenty-First Year

St. Petersburg, Florida, Tuesday, April 16, 1912

Price, 3 Cents   Number. 95

Titantic Sinks With 1,530 Souls Aboard

OROZOO'S MEN ARE PUT TO FLIGHT BY FEDERAL TROOPS

TAFT'S FORCES ARE STAGGERED BY PENNA. DEFEAT

MONSTER LEVIATHAN SUNK AT 2:30 MONDAY, EXACTING AWFUL TOLL OF LIFE

COMMERCIAL CLUB "CHEWS THE RAG" ON WATERFRONT

LEVEES STILL BRAKING ALONG LOWER RIVER

Greatest Vessel Ever Built in the History of the World Was on Maiden Voyage from Liverpool to New York---Carried 2,200 People Including Crew---Only 670 Escape With Their Lives---Was Due to Arrive in New York Today.

GREAT DISASTER OF YESTERDAY ECLIPSES THAT OF THE GENERAL SLOCUM OF SEVERAL YEARS AGO

All Women and Children Crowded Into Small Life Boats and Are Picked Up by Str. Carpathia, Which Is First to Reach Scene of Great Disaster---Captain of Carpathia Confirms by Wireless Sinking of Great Vessel.

" History Made..., January 2, 1914

"History was made in St. Petersburg yesterday…the flight of Tony Jannus and his passenger, ex-Mayor, A.C. Pheil, yesterday morning from St. Petersburg to Tampa opening the first line of flying craft to be established in the world for commercial purposes."

ABOVE: Washington's Birthday parade in St. Petersburg, 1915. The annual event later became the Festival of States.
Courtesy Heritage Village Archives & Library

TOP LEFT: Tony Jannus in the Benoist Airboat *Old 43.* This plane was put into service during the summer of 1913, practicing and perfecting the scheduled run that the "World's First Scheduled Commercial Airline" planned to make after the inauguration of the airboat line on Jan. 1, 1914. *Courtesy City of St. Petersburg*

LEFT: E.A. Marshall family and their two Model T Fords, Dunedin, circa 1910. From left are Mr. E.A. Marshall, Mrs. E.A. Marshall, Scott A. Marshall, E. Conrad Marshall, Alfred P. Marshall and Emily F. Marshall (Mrs. Ella Kromling). *Courtesy Heritage Village Archives & Library*

"To Some Correspondents, May 15, 1916

"The *Times* has received several communications upon the *Lusitania* disaster. All good citizens must and will do what they can to hold up the hands of our great and wise and just president, and the *Times* does not care to publish any communications upon war questions or issues that do not follow his lead during this stage of the great crisis."

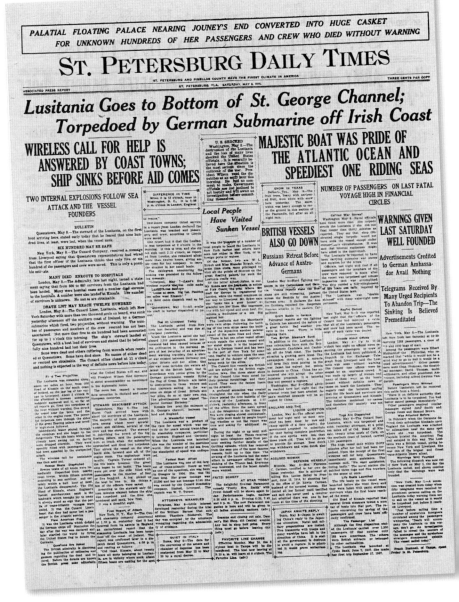

ST. PETERSBURG DAILY TIMES

Lusitania Goes to Bottom of St. George Channel; Torpedoed by German Submarine off Irish Coast

WIRELESS CALL FOR HELP IS ANSWERED BY COAST TOWNS; SHIP SINKS BEFORE AID COMES

MAJESTIC BOAT WAS PRIDE OF THE ATLANTIC OCEAN AND SPEEDIEST ONE RIDING SEAS

WARNINGS GIVEN LAST SATURDAY WELL FOUNDED

ABOVE: Front page of the *St. Petersburg Daily Times*, May 8, 1915. *Courtesy Special Collections and Archives, Nelson Poynter Memorial Library, University of South Florida St. Petersburg*

TOP LEFT: Boiling cane syrup in the Tarpon Springs area, circa 1915. *Courtesy Heritage Village Archives & Library*

LEFT: Afraid that St. Petersburg would try to become the seat of the new Pinellas County, a Clearwater group hastily built what came to be called the "overnight courthouse" in 1912. Most of the infant county's elected officials posed for this photo, including Dixie M. Hollins, the first superintendent of schools (far right). *Courtesy Heritage Village Archives & Library*

OPPOSITE: Three Friends Cigar Co. and Mims Transfer on E Scott Street, with employees in wagons in front, Tampa, 1915. *Courtesy Tampa-Hillsborough County Public Library System*

ABOVE: Wintersgill's band on the Gulfport and St. Petersburg Local Express wagon, circa 1918. The driver is Washington Wintersgill, and Bryan Coleman is one of the young men behind the driver. Jesse Coleman is wearing a white shirt next to the band leader, O.E. Palmiter. *Courtesy Heritage Village Archives & Library*

LEFT: Front page of the *St. Petersburg Daily Times*, March 9, 1916. *Courtesy Special Collections and Archives, Nelson Poynter Memorial Library, University of South Florida St. Petersburg*

OPPOSITE: Tractor pulling a log train for R.E. Olds Farm Co. in Oldsmar, 1916. *Courtesy Tampa-Hillsborough County Public Library System*

BOTTOM LEFT: Three of the earliest businesses in New Port Richey. This photo, from 1915 or shortly thereafter, shows the Hotel Newport, the Port Richey Lumber and Hardware Co., and the New Port Richey Drugstore. These buildings were on the east side of what is now Grand Boulevard, between Main Street and Orange Lake. The Hotel Newport was constructed in 1914 by Anthony J. Pauels, who later became a New Port Richey City Council member, and Mike Broersma. Both men came from Michigan. Michael and Minnie Broersma came to Port Richey in February 1914 and ran the hotel until 1920, when they moved to Sarasota. *Courtesy Archives of the St. Petersburg Times*

ABOVE: Mayor Al Lang, circa 1920. Lang served as mayor from 1916 to 1920, and later gained fame as St. Petersburg's unofficial "ambassador of baseball." *Courtesy Archives of the St. Petersburg Times*

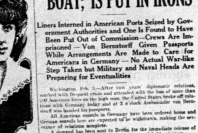

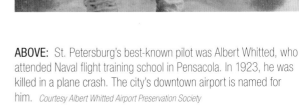

ABOVE: St. Petersburg's best-known pilot was Albert Whitted, who attended Naval flight training school in Pensacola. In 1923, he was killed in a plane crash. The city's downtown airport is named for him. *Courtesy Albert Whitted Airport Preservation Society*

LEFT: Front page of the *St. Petersburg Daily Times*, February 4, 1917. *Courtesy Special Collections and Archives, Nelson Poynter Memorial Library, University of South Florida St. Petersburg*

ABOVE: Southern College baseball team with A.O. Burleson listed as one of the players, Sutherland (now Palm Harbor), circa 1919. In 1922, the college moved to Lakeland, and in 1935, it was renamed Florida Southern College. *Courtesy Heritage Village Archives & Library*

LEFT: One-time *Times* owner A.C. Turner with five of his children, February 1918. From left, front row, A. Fred Turner (a Methodist minister), A.C. Turner and David B. Turner, former *Times* printer and longtime editor-publisher of a newspaper in Bulloch County, Ga. Back row, Mrs. Mamie Turner Crane of Tampa, Mrs. Estelle Turner Converse (once worked for the *Atlanta Journal*) and Mrs. Carrie Turner Nelson. *Courtesy Archives of the St. Petersburg Times*

BOTTOM LEFT: Parade on Zack Street in Tampa, at the 400-600 blocks, honoring World War I draftees, September 1917. *Courtesy Tampa-Hillsborough County Public Library System*

BELOW: Girls basketball team from St. Petersburg High School, circa 1918. From left, Valeta Brown, Harriet Endicott, Mary Elizabeth Foster, Ada Boyer, Nell Williams, Cecile Hubbell, Bessie Dew, Frances Proctor, Gladys Osborn and coach Marguerite Blocker. *Courtesy Heritage Village Archives & Library*

RIGHT: Passengers ride the Tampa-Clearwater bus, 1919. Notice the World War I honor roll in the background at left. *Courtesy Heritage Village Archives & Library*

OPPOSITE TOP: Crowds gather on the dock with swimmers just off the shore at a Fourth of July celebration in Oldsmar, 1919. *Courtesy Tampa-Hillsborough County Public Library System*

BELOW: Shipbuilding at Oscar Daniels Co. on the east side of the Estuary Zone in Tampa, circa 1919. *Courtesy Tampa-Hillsborough County Public Library System*

BOTTOM: A view of downtown Tampa from the top of City Hall, looking north, circa 1919. *Courtesy Tampa-Hillsborough County Public Library System*

The 1920s

America's factories and farms flourished during World War I. And when the war ended in late 1918, many people had spending money, a yen to see America and a new way to do it – in one of Henry Ford's inexpensive Model Ts. Thousands of them came to the Tampa Bay area, which from 1920 to 1926 saw a dizzying real estate boom that transformed the region.

There was also a hurricane. It roared ashore on Oct. 25, 1921, inundating low-lying areas, beaching boats, obliterating buildings and washing out bridges. The worst storm since 1848 proved to be a temporary setback, however. Amid the widespread destruction, the *Times* reported, "there stood … Gibraltar-like, the indomitable will, spirit and energy that had made St. Petersburg the queen of the West Coast of Florida, whose right to reign supreme remains undisputed."

On both sides of the bay, there was a frenzy of real estate speculation, with property rapidly changing hands multiple times. New subdivisions sprang up, like Davis Islands and Golden Hills (later Temple Terrace) in Hillsborough and Snell Isle and Allendale in St. Petersburg. Both cities got new hotels. Tampa's municipal hospital (now Tampa General) moved to Davis Islands, and St. Petersburg got a Coliseum for big bands and a new pier financed by a million-dollar bond issue. By the end of the decade, St. Petersburg's population had grown from 14,237 to 40,425 (down from an estimated 60,000 in 1926), Clearwater's from 2,247 to 7,607, and Tampa's from 51,608 to 101,161.

No public project was more important than construction of the 2 ½-mile Gandy Bridge, which opened in 1924. A 43-mile drive from St. Petersburg to Tampa was now only 19 miles. It ended St. Petersburg's isolation in a world that, thanks to the advent of radio, was already beginning to shrink. The first station in Florida was WDAE in Tampa, which began broadcasting in 1922.

It took a lot of workers to build the houses, hotels, public buildings and roads. Many of the laborers were black men, some of whom had come from rural Florida, Alabama and Georgia. Vital though they were to the economy, black families got few benefits of the boom. Most lived in shabby homes in rigidly segregated neighborhoods that lacked paved streets, plumbing and electricity.

The *Times* feasted on the boom. In 1925, only one newspaper in America – the *Miami Herald* – had more lines of advertising. In 1926, the *Times* published a special promotion edition of 19 sections and 232 pages. At one point, it ran out of newsprint and had to print a Sunday edition on pink paper it got from the *Tampa Times*.

The boom ended in 1926 almost as quickly as it began. Then came the stock market crash of 1929 and the Great Depression, which would have calamitous consequences for Tampa Bay.

LEFT: Three golfers enjoy a sunny day at the Sunset Golf and Country Club on Snell Isle in St. Petersburg, circa 1925. The club is the oldest city course still in use. *Courtesy Archives of the St. Petersburg Times*

Women's Votes, July 1, 1920

"Suffrage is not a question of political parties, but of citizenship. Whatever the mistaken ideas or false hopes of either male or female politicians may be, when the clean-cut, thinking American woman gets the vote, she will accept it not as a bribe, but as her right, and she will use it as her conscience and her judgment dictate."

ABOVE: Manuel Corral and Francisco Sierra stand by their automobiles in front of the Corral, Wodiska and Co. Factory No. 8 at 2612 14th St., Ybor City, 1921. *Courtesy Tampa-Hillsborough County Public Library System*

TOP LEFT: A view of Tampa and the Hillsborough River, circa 1920.
Courtesy Tampa-Hillsborough County Public Library System

BOTTOM LEFT: An entry in the Festival of States parade in St. Petersburg, circa 1920.
Courtesy Heritage Village Archives & Library

OPPOSITE BOTTOM LEFT: The Pheil Hotel, right, was under construction when this shot was taken in the early 1920s in St. Petersburg. The Old Central National Bank, left, was decorated for the Festival of States parade. *Courtesy Archives of the St. Petersburg Times*

OPPOSITE BOTTOM RIGHT: Street scene in Oldsmar, circa 1920. *Courtesy Heritage Village Archives & Library*

Pinellas Storm, October 27, 1921

"... the storm which swept Pinellas Peninsula was a severe one and the damage it did was great. It was the newspaper's duty to furnish this news to the people as completely and as thoroughly as it was able to do even under the adverse circumstances. And we are publishing a newspaper."

ABOVE: On October 25, 1921, the Tampa Bay area took a direct hit from a hurricane that had sprung up in the western Caribbean. The wind and tidal surge left widespread destruction. The waterfronts of both St. Petersburg and Tampa were littered with the debris of sunken and disabled boats like this one in Tampa. *Courtesy State Archives collection*

OPPOSITE: The sponge exchange in Tarpon Springs, circa 1920. In the group is George M. Emmanuel, first independent buyer and lobbyist in Washington for protective sponge tariffs and second president of the Tarpon Springs Sponge Exchange. *Courtesy Archives of the St. Petersburg Times*

BELOW: The hurricane left the 4-year-old Yacht Club in downtown St. Petersburg engulfed by water. *Courtesy Heritage Village Archives & Library*

STORM — St. Petersburg Times — EXTRA

St. Petersburg, Fla., Wednesday Morning, Oct. 26, 1921

TROPICAL STORM SWEEPS CITY

Property Damage May Reach $5,000,000; Two Men Die

RUMOR PASS-A-GRILLE WIPED OUT

With property loss estimated at $5,000,000, and two known dead, the water front a sea of debris and sunken ships, St. Petersburg Tuesday was swept by the worst tropical storm in the history of the West coast, striking about 3 o'clock in the morning and lasting until late in the afternoon, unroofing hundreds of hotels, apartment houses and homes, tearing down power lines and isolating the city completely from the outside world.

Communication was completely cut off from Pass-a-Grille, where reports estimated the loss of life from 15 to 150, with the resort under five feet of water.

ABOVE: Front page of the *St. Petersburg Times*, October 26, 1921. The storm destroyed two wooden bridges to the Pinellas beaches. With Pass-a-Grille beach and its 200 residents cut off from the mainland and no way to get information, the *Times* breathlessly reported what it had — rumors. A few hours later, the paper published a second extra edition with a dramatically different headline. *Courtesy Archives of the St. Petersburg Times*

ABOVE: View of Cleveland Street and Garden Avenue intersection in Clearwater, looking west, 1921. Visible in the photo are the Richardson Building and Coachman Building. *Courtesy Heritage Village Archives & Library*

BELOW: This man, called the "Human Fly" in the early 1920s, performed daring stunts on the Princess Martha Hotel in downtown St. Petersburg, circa 1921. *Courtesy Archives of the St. Petersburg Times*

"Talking to London, October 7, 1922

"When Marconi first perfected his wireless telegraph and it became possible to transmit messages through this medium, it was considered that he had accomplished all that could be possible in that line, but from that time the proficiency of aerial communication service has advanced until, on last Saturday, a concert given in Newark, NJ was heard in London, England.

The Newark test established for the first time the possibility of trans-Atlantic communication by this means.

It is good to live in this age of progress."

ABOVE: Harrison Hardware Co. on Central Avenue, east of Ninth Street in St. Petersburg. This store was a branch operation and owned by Ernest Cunningham, who for many years was sheriff of Pinellas County. *Courtesy Heritage Village Archives & Library*

OPPOSITE: Tampa Smokers baseball team at Plant Field in Tampa, April 1922. *Courtesy Tampa-Hillsborough County Public Library System*

RIGHT: Clearwater firefighters at the fire station and City Hall building, 1922. This building at Laura Street and N Fort Harrison Avenue was built in 1911. Ora S. Hart, chief; Bill McKillip, Walter Lovell, "Shorty" Mitchell, Joe Russell, Art Geiselman and George Bolton. *Courtesy Heritage Village Archives & Library*

BELOW: Students and staff at Tampa Business College at the northwest corner of Grand Central Avenue and Edison Street, Tampa, circa 1922. *Courtesy Tampa-Hillsborough County Public Library System*

ABOUT: Child and men with a 1906 Maxwell car in front of United Motor Co. on the 1700 block of Franklin Street in Tampa, 1923.
Courtesy Tampa-Hillsborough County Public Library System

RIGHT: The Gulf High School basketball team in the mid 1920s. New Port Richey's Gulf High School played its first basketball games during the 1923-24 school year, the second year the school was in operation. *Courtesy Archives of the St. Petersburg Times*

Gandy Bridge, November 20, 1924

"The great Gandy Bridge has been completed and today will be formally opened with interesting and appropriate ceremonies. What the great bridge will mean in the development of this section, and what a convenience and pleasure it will prove is difficult to foreshadow, since the structure is built to endure and each year will become of more value."

ABOVE: George S. Gandy built the first bridge that linked the Pinellas peninsula to Tampa, effectively ending St. Petersburg's isolation from the rest of Florida. *Courtesy Archives of the St. Petersburg Times*

TOP LEFT: The east end of the bridge starts across the bay in September 1923. To the right is a temporary construction pier. *Courtesy Archives of the St. Petersburg Times*

LEFT: Front page of the *St. Petersburg Times*, November 20, 1924, which marked the opening of the Gandy Bridge. *Courtesy Special Collections and Archives, Nelson Poynter Memorial Library, University of South Florida St. Petersburg*

FAR LEFT: "World's Largest Checkerboard" in Municipal Park, Clearwater, circa 1923. *Courtesy Heritage Village Archives & Library*

ABOVE: D.P. Davis, the developer who created Davis Islands out of two marshy keys, looks across the bay. He is wearing knickers (sometimes called "acreage britches"), the uniform of many real estate salesmen during the 1920s boom. *Courtesy University of South Florida Special Collections*

RIGHT: In 1924, dredging begins for Davis Islands just south of downtown Tampa. *Courtesy University of South Florida Special Collections*

ABOVE: The home of Eugene Elliott in the Coffee Pot Bayou section of St. Petersburg, circa 1924. A real estate tycoon, Elliott helped raise money for the construction of the Gandy Bridge and then purchased most of Weedon Island, just south of the new bridge on the Pinellas side of the bay. The development was never completed. Elliott went bankrupt, accidentally killed his wife during a dispute on the steps of their home and left the city in disgrace. *Courtesy Tampa-Hillsborough County Public Library System*

LEFT: *St. Petersburg Times* editor Edwin E. Naugle was a baseball fan. During the 1924 World Series, a crowd gathered around the *Times* office at First Avenue S and Fifth Street to "watch" the game. Play-by-play information, which reached the newsroom by telegraph, would be relayed to the crowd by Naugle through a megaphone, then posted on a "Playograph." *Courtesy Archives of the St. Petersburg Times*

BELOW: Tampa Electric Co. streetcar on Grand Central Avenue near the Tampa Bay Hotel in August 1925. *Courtesy Tampa-Hillsborough County Public Library System*

ABOVE: People and cars in front of First Baptist Church, northeast corner of Plant and Eagle streets, Tampa, circa 1925.
Courtesy Tampa-Hillsborough County Public Library System

RIGHT: As a copy boy and cub reporter in 1923-24, Tom Harris wore knickers. When he became a full-fledged reporter, a colleague bought him a pair of long pants. Harris became managing editor in 1933, executive editor in 1941. *Courtesy Archives of the St. Petersburg Times*

FAR RIGHT: During the boom years of the 1920s, the *St. Petersburg Times* grew dramatically in both circulation and staff. The paper moved into a new building in 1926 and 1927. *Courtesy Special Collections and Archives, Nelson Poynter Memorial Library, University of South Florida St. Petersburg*

"The *Times* is printed on pink paper today, not because of any festive occasion or because of any unusual event, but because the business of the *Times* is such that it has become a matter of considerable trouble to get enough paper to care for the large business now enjoyed by the *Times*."

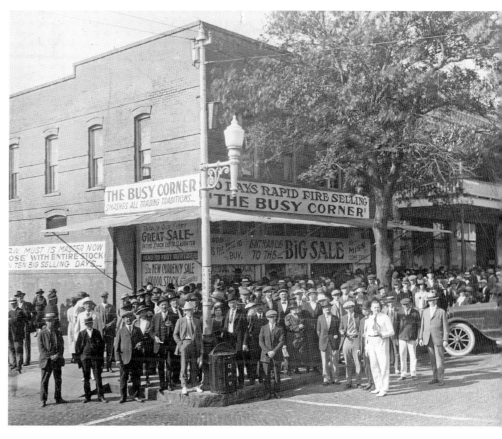

ABOVE: Crowds gather at The Busy Corner at Central Avenue and Third Street during a "Big Sale" as advertised on the building, 1920s. *Courtesy Archives of the St. Petersburg Times*

TOP LEFT: The first new hotel in downtown St. Petersburg was the Soreno, which opened on January 1, 1924. Like the Vinoy and other stylish hotels and restaurants, the Soreno barred Jewish guests, according to historian Raymond Arsenault. In 1992, the hotel was imploded, a scene filmed for the movie *Lethal Weapon 3*. The Florencia condominium tower now stands on the site. *Courtesy Archives of the St. Petersburg Times*

LEFT: The distinctive pink Don CeSar Hotel rises from the sands of Pass-a-Grille in June 1926. The Don, which opened in 1928, was one of 10 big hotels built in southern Pinellas County during the 1920s boom. It became a military hospital in 1942, then became a Veterans Administration office building after the war. It was vacated by the federal government in 1969 and lay vacant until it was restored and reopened as a hotel in 1973. *Courtesy Archives of the St. Petersburg Times*

ABOVE: Streetcar, automobile and pedestrian traffic on Franklin Street in Tampa, between the 600 and 700 blocks, looking northeast toward the Exchange National Bank, 1925. *Courtesy Tampa-Hillsborough County Public Library System*

TOP RIGHT: Gray Moss Inn at 201 S Fort Harrison Ave., Clearwater, circa 1925. *Courtesy Tampa-Hillsborough County Public Library System*

BOTTOM RIGHT: Children pose in front of Tampa's library for black residents, 1922. *Courtesy Jack B. Moore, University of South Florida*

BELOW: Val's Corner on the northeast corner of Lafayette and Tampa streets, 1924. *Courtesy Tampa-Hillsborough County Public Library System*

ABOVE: Florida Avenue looking north from Tampa City Hall, with a view of Tampa Terrace Hotel and Sacred Heart Catholic Church, 1926. *Courtesy Tampa-Hillsborough County Public Library System*

BELOW: Original Czechoslovakian settlers of Masaryktown in Hernando County pose on a piece of land that is now off U.S. 41 S, September 1925. The small sign above the American flag reads, "VITAME VAS!" It's Czechoslovakian for "We welcome you!" *Courtesy State Archives Collection*

ABOVE: Agricultural workers labor in a commercial tomato field in Ruskin, 1926. *Courtesy Tampa-Hillsborough County Public Library System*

BELOW: Motorists drive on Tampa's Bayshore Boulevard, 1926. *Courtesy State Archives Collection*

OPPOSITE: Not only did children enjoy swinging from the bars, but also grownups would try out their skills at Spa Beach in St. Petersburg in the 1920s. The Vinoy Hotel can be seen in the distance. *Courtesy Archives of the St. Petersburg Times*

BELOW: Crowds gather for a golf game in the 1920s at the Bear Creek Country Club (later called the Pasadena Golf and County Club). Bear Creek attracted golf stars like Bobby Jones and Gene Sarazen, and the flamboyant Walter Hagen was the club's pro and president for two years in the mid 1920s. *Courtesy Archives of the St. Petersburg Times*

ABOVE: In the 1920s when the end of school was in sight, St. Petersburg Beach was the place to take the children for an outing and picnic. *Courtesy Archives of the St. Petersburg Times*

BELOW: Finding a place to park was always difficult at the Municipal Pier, St. Petersburg, 1920s. *Courtesy Archives of the St. Petersburg Times*

ABOVE: Good Humor refrigerated ice cream vending truck in Tampa, 1926. *Courtesy Tampa-Hillsborough County Public Library System*

LEFT: Automobile show display sponsored by Tampa Auto Dealers Association at the Davis Islands Coliseum in 1926.
Courtesy Tampa-Hillsborough County Public Library System

BELOW: Crowds gather to watch heavyweight boxing champion Jack Dempsey in action in Tampa on February 4, 1926.
Courtesy Tampa-Hillsborough County Public Library System

ABOVE: Business street with stores and a café in Brooksville, 1926. *Courtesy Tampa-Hillsborough County Public Library System*

TOP LEFT: Tampa Fire Department pumper and firefighters supporting the Community Chest drive in front of the Tampa courthouse, 1926. *Courtesy Tampa-Hillsborough County Public Library System*

BOTTOM LEFT: View of First Street S and the St. Petersburg waterfront, looking south, circa 1925. *Courtesy Archives of the St. Petersburg Times*

BELOW: Public officials stand by the first car to drive over the 22nd Street Causeway in Tampa, January 22, 1926.
Courtesy Tampa-Hillsborough County Public Library System

ABOVE: Crowd gathers for a land sale at Golden Hills in Hillsborough County in March 1926.
Courtesy Tampa-Hillsborough County Public Library System

RIGHT: Rooftop view of the Festival of States floats and parade moving west on Central Avenue in St. Petersburg, 1926. *Courtesy Tampa-Hillsborough County Public Library System*

ABOVE: Members from San Remo Club ride a float during the Festival of States, spring of 1926.
Courtesy Heritage Village Archives & Library

LEFT: Workers crate strawberries in an open-sided warehouse in Plant City, 1926.
Courtesy Tampa-Hillsborough County Public Library System

BELOW: The St. Petersburg waterfront and Municipal Marina, circa 1926.
Courtesy Tampa-Hillsborough County Public Library System

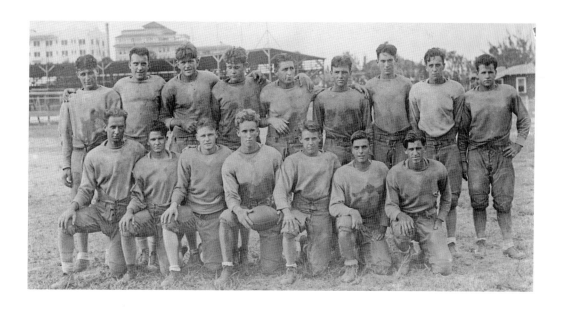

ABOVE: The St. Petersburg High School football team, 1926-27. This photo was taken in Waterfront Park. *Courtesy Archives of the St. Petersburg Times*

TOP LEFT: Front page of the *St. Petersburg Times*, May 21, 1927. *Courtesy Special Collections and Archives, Nelson Poynter Memorial Library, University of South Florida St. Petersburg*

BOTTOM LEFT: The Bayou at Tarpon Springs, early 1920s. *Courtesy Archives of the St. Petersburg Times*

OPPOSITE: Tourists and local citizens relax on the famous green benches. This photo, circa 1926, looks south from Fifth Street N toward Central Avenue. St. Petersburg was known as the city of green benches, and there were scores of them throughout the city. The city fathers did away with them in the 1960s, concerned that they created a geriatric image. *Courtesy Archives of the St. Petersburg Times*

BELOW: The Royal Poinciana Band, composed of area residents and sponsored by the Turner-Brandon American Legion Post in Clearwater, circa 1926. The band, under the direction of Professor Thomas Altobellis, made its debut on Labor Day 1926. *Courtesy Heritage Village Archives & Library*

ABOVE: Festival of States queen coronation at Williams Park in St. Petersburg, circa 1927. *Courtesy Tampa-Hillsborough County Public Library System*

LEFT: During spring training in the late 1920s in St. Petersburg, New York Yankees legend Babe Ruth shows his batting grip to two fans believed to be Mike and Ike, twin midgets with the Johnny J. Jones Exposition, a local carnival. The Yankees moved the training camp to St. Petersburg from New Orleans in 1925. When reporters asked Ruth what he thought of St. Petersburg, he replied, "If anyone can have fun in this town, I can." As for Mike and Ike, Matthew "Mike" Matina and Bela "Ike" Matina later played Munchkins in the 1939 classic *The Wizard of Oz* and remain the shortest twins on record, a 2 feet 6 inches tall. *Courtesy Archives of the St. Petersburg Times*

BELOW: The 1927 New York Yankees at spring training in St. Petersburg. Considered by many to be one of the greatest baseball teams of all time, the Yankees won 110 games en route to a World Series sweep of the Pittsburgh Pirates. The team featured future Hall of Famers such as Babe Ruth, Lou Gehrig, Herb Pennock, Waite Hoyt, Earle Combs and Tony Lazzeri. *Courtesy Tampa-Hillsborough County Public Library System*

ABOVE: St. Petersburg Automobile Dealers Association picnic at Indian Rocks Beach, circa 1927. *Courtesy Tampa-Hillsborough County Public Library System*

RIGHT: A view of Main Street in New Port Richey during the boom period in the 1920s. The building on the left side of the street with awnings is the Chasco Inn building, although when this photo was taken it was the Harmony Hotel. Constructed in 1915, it is the oldest existing building in New Port Richey. The old water tower can be seen behind it. The building on the extreme right of the photo, sometimes called the Milbauer building, was the first brick building in town. It was built in 1919. *Courtesy Archives of the St. Petersburg Times*

BELOW: The first graduating class from Largo High School, 1927. Students are, front row from left, Golding Whittie Rothermel, Frances Schwartz, Mattie Lou Brown, Catherine Coit (adviser), Kathryn Mixon Nichols, Virginia Grable Brown and Ruby Jean Campbell Gaunt. Middle row, Oswald Laurence, Victor Schultz, Evelyn Powell, Louise Terry, Mattie Mae McMullen Johnson, Robert Jackson and Sheldon Walsingham. Back row, Marcus Fields, Reuel McLaughlin and Brenton" Chum" Dewar. *Courtesy Archives of the St. Petersburg Times*

ABOVE: Children and workers pose at a nursery school run by the Tampa Urban League, 1922. *Courtesy Tampa-Hillsborough County Public Library System*

Times Platform, 1928

"St. Petersburg – Florida's Best City: The Tourist Metropolis – the City Beautiful – municipal planning – unification of railroads and harbor terminals – public ownership of all public utilities – better street parking – more parks – playgrounds – recreation areas – boulevards – bay shore and lakeside drives – development of Gulf beaches – a non-partisan, non-political, business methods city government."

ABOVE: Ore train on an access track in a Brooksville open-pit strip mine, 1928. *Courtesy Tampa-Hillsborough County Public Library System*

TOP RIGHT: Cigar sorters and binders at work at Berriman Brothers in Tampa, 1929. *Courtesy Tampa-Hillsborough County Public Library System*

RIGHT: A. Cappello and Brother Grocery Store, located at 213 W Fortune St. in Tampa, 1928. *Courtesy Archives of the St. Petersburg Times*

OPPOSITE TOP: Brandon High School graduating class of 1928. *Courtesy Tampa-Hillsborough County Public Library System*

OPPOSITE BOTTOM: A Waterfront Park spring training baseball game between the Philadelphia Athletics and the Boston Braves, St. Petersburg, circa 1927. *Courtesy Tampa-Hillsborough County Public Library System*

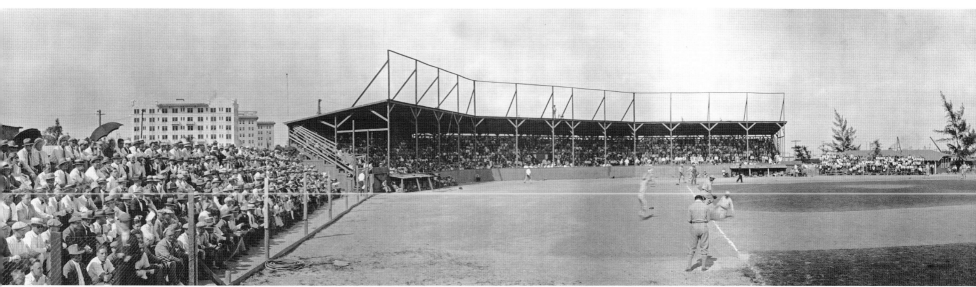

ABOVE: Couples dance at the American Legion Hell Harbor Ball at Davis Islands Coliseum in Tampa, 1929.
Courtesy Tampa-Hillsborough County Public Library System

TOP LEFT: Front page of the *St. Petersburg Times*, February 15, 1929. *Courtesy Special Collections and Archives, Nelson Poynter Memorial Library, University of South Florida St. Petersburg*

LEFT: Construction of a dirigible hangar (which sheltered a Goodyear blimp) at Albert Whitted Airport, St. Petersburg, circa 1929. *Courtesy Heritage Village Archives & Library*

OPPOSITE: In the late 1920s, cruising around the pierhead and strolling along the Municipal Pier in St. Petersburg were popular activities. *Courtesy Archives of the St. Petersburg Times*

FOLLOWING: Atlantic Coast Line workers with locomotive in Tampa, circa 1929. According to the *Evening Independent* of March 22, 1929, the locomotive shops in Tampa were the largest and most modern in the South and had a capacity of 50 locomotives. They employed 500 men then and up to 1,500 at peak business. *Courtesy Tampa-Hillsborough County Public Library System*

The 1930s

The dark days of the Great Depression were a grim time for the Tampa Bay area. Money and credit dried up. Tourism fell dramatically. Thousands lost their jobs. Banks weakened, then collapsed. Anxiety and interracial tension grew.

The city of St. Petersburg defaulted on millions of dollars in bond payments, and the Pinellas School Board laid off its maintenance staff, turned out the lights at all schools except during emergencies and, for a time, even charged tuition. Money grew so short in St. Petersburg that a Citizens Emergency Committee issued scrip that could be used in lieu of cash. Many employers paid their workers at least partly in scrip, which was honored by merchants all over town.

Even gangsters had a hard time. The city filed tax liens against property owned by Al Capone and three associates in 1936. Agents for the mobster, who was in prison for tax evasion, made the payments two months later.

At least St. Petersburg didn't descend into rampant lawlessness like two of its neighbors. In Brooksville, City Attorney Herbert Smithson – believed by some to be helping federal agents identify rumrunners – was gunned down in front of a hotel by three men wielding shotguns. No one was ever prosecuted for his murder. In Tampa, bolita – the illegal numbers game – became

such big business that both politicians and police were on the take. Rival gangs clashed repeatedly and several men were killed. Then in a 1935 mayoral primary, there were 3,000 more votes cast than there were voters. Two men were shot and 50 arrested for tampering with the election.

Amid the upheavals and economic stagnation, new Depression-era public works efforts produced some important projects and jobs for thousands. St. Petersburg got a new city hall, a new Coast Guard air base and a big veterans hospital and administration center. Using federal funds, the city bought 26 acres and built the Jordan Park public housing complex for black residents in 1939.

A bridge company run by Ben T. Davis used a big loan from the Reconstruction Finance Corp. to build a bridge (now called the Courtney Campbell Parkway) from Tampa to Clearwater. Tampa got the Peter O. Knight Airport, Fort Homer Hesterly Armory and a new 7,000-foot asphalt runway for Drew Field (now Tampa International Airport). In 1939, federal officials announced plans to build MacDill Field (now MacDill Air Force Base) at the southern end of the peninsula.

The Depression hit the *Times* hard. Advertising revenue plummeted, and the size of the staff and the paper shrank dramatically. Paul Poynter's outside business ventures were struggling, too, so the paper took on new partners. In 1935, some of them wrested control of the paper from Poynter and, in effect, kicked him out of the building. It took seven weeks – and the support of family, friends and advertisers – for Poynter to regain control.

LEFT: Members of a St. Petersburg carpenters union protest the payment of low non-union wages by local construction companies, 1938. *Courtesy Archives of the St. Petersburg Times*

77

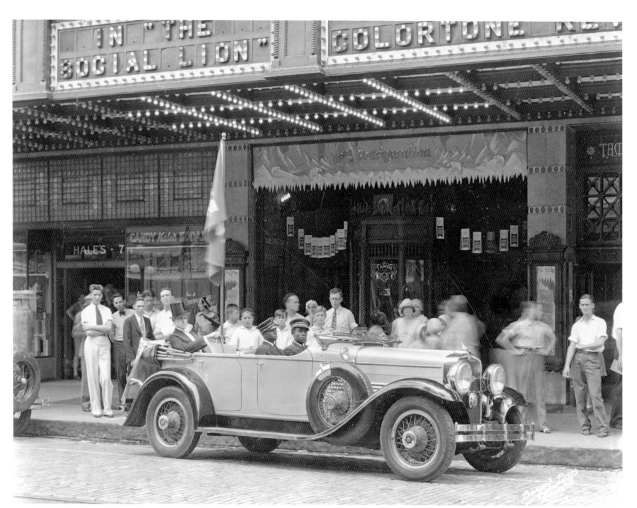

ABOVE: Burts Hardware Co., at 1106 Franklin St., and Vickers Printing Co., at 1110½ Franklin St., in Tampa, with a Coca-Cola billboard, 1930. *Courtesy Tampa-Hillsborough County Public Library System*

TOP LEFT: Automobile shipment for R.S. Evans, arriving and unloaded from the *Gomal* at the Mallory Dock in Tampa, 1930. *Courtesy Tampa-Hillsborough County Public Library System*

BOTTOM LEFT: Actor Jackie Oakie (wearing tophat) appears at the Tampa Theatre at 707 Franklin St. on June 19, 1930. He appeared in *The Social Lion*, which was playing at the theater. *Courtesy Tampa-Hillsborough County Public Library System*

BELOW: Construction of Firestone Service Stores Inc., with tower scaffolding. The store was built on 900 E Lafayette St., in Tampa, 1930. *Courtesy Tampa-Hillsborough County Public Library System*

ABOVE: Drilling operation in rural Hillsborough County, 1930. *Courtesy Tampa-Hillsborough County Public Library System*

TOP LEFT: Croquet players and spectators under shade trees at Plant Park in Tampa in the spring of 1930. *Courtesy Tampa-Hillsborough County Public Library System*

BOTTOM LEFT: Central Avenue and Fifth Street, St. Petersburg, 1930s. Note the sign touting "X-ray shoes." *Courtesy Archives of the St. Petersburg Times*

BELOW: Construction of addition to Federal Building basement floor and stone exterior, at Twiggs and Zack streets, 1930. *Courtesy Tampa-Hillsborough County Public Library System*

After 30 Years, April 1, 1931

"April 1, 1901, just 30 years ago this day, W.L. Straub and two associates bought the *St. Petersburg Times*.

Thirty years ago St. Petersburg wasn't much. The railroad narrow gauge from Sanford had arrived in 1888, and in 1890 the United States census taken counted 273 persons here. In 1900 – one year before that April 1, 1901 – he had counted 1,575. The *Times* was not only bought on April 1, but the price paid was $1,300 – we don't remember if it was a Friday or not.

The St. Petersburg of today tells its own story of dreams and the hopes and the struggles that brought into being the city we have."

ABOVE: The automobile age unofficially arrives in Tampa Bay with a new brand of tourists. Starting in the winter of 1919-20, thousands of visitors settled into camp grounds instead of hotels. They were called "tin can tourists" because they ate a lot of canned goods and sometimes patched their mufflers with empty cans. Most camps, like this one in Hillsborough County, circa 1930, were on private land. In St. Petersburg, hundreds of people camped on city land at 18th Street and Second Avenue S for a time before the City Council abolished it in 1921. *Courtesy Tampa-Hillsborough County Public Library System*

LEFT: Miss America and America's Healthiest Girl with their pilot, shortly after arriving in Clearwater, 1930.
Courtesy Tampa-Hillsborough County Public Library System

BELOW: Whiskey caches at 1014 10th Ave. in Tampa after being uncovered by authorities during Prohibition in 1931. The 18th Amendment, which took effect in 1920, banned the sale, manufacture and transportation of alchol for consumption. It was repealed with ratification of the 21st Amendment on December 5, 1933. *Courtesy Tampa-Hillsborough County Public Library System*

ABOVE: An audience gathers for the dedication ceremony of the Salvation Army facility in Hillsborough County, November 1931.
Courtesy Tampa-Hillsborough County Public Library System

TOP RIGHT: A streetcar advertises Dr. M. Sayle Taylor's "Married Love" lecture at the Strand Theatre in 1931. *Courtesy Tampa-Hillsborough County Public Library System*

BOTTOM RIGHT: Florida Avenue looking south from Zack Street to Tampa Terrace Hotel, 1930. *Courtesy Tampa-Hillsborough County Public Library System*

ABOVE: Depositors lined up like this at banks from Tallahassee to Key West in 1931. The Florida boom of 1920-26 had ended, and the public awoke to closed banks, heavy public debt and ruined investors. This photo is of the second run on Central National Bank in St. Petersburg.
Courtesy Archives of the St. Petersburg Times

TOP RIGHT: Miss Florida poses in her swimsuit for a promotion in front of the Joyland Silver Dome at Clearwater Beach, 1931.
Courtesy Tampa-Hillsborough County Public Library System

BOTTOM RIGHT: Exhausted dancers are examined by dance marathon judges, 1932. Dance marathons, which got their start in the 1920s, were also known as "bunion derbies" and "corn and callus carnivals." *Courtesy Tampa-Hillsborough County Public Library System*

OPPOSITE: A couple canoe in Homosassa Springs, 1932. *Courtesy Tampa-Hillsborough County Public Library System*

BELOW: Commercial fishermen ply their net on the beach in Pass-a-Grille, 1931. *Courtesy Tampa-Hillsborough County Public Library System*

ABOVE: The Goodyear blimp *Reliance* awaits action at Albert Whitted Airport on the St. Petersburg waterfront in 1932. Dirigibles were all the rage when the City Council appropriated $33,062 for a blimp hangar there in 1929. Blimps remained at the airport for more than a decade.
Courtesy Archives of the St. Petersburg Times

BELOW: A crowd enjoys the sand and surf at Clearwater Beach in the 1930s. *Courtesy Tampa-Hillsborough County Public Library System*

ABOVE: The Tampa College football team poses for a portrait on the football field in 1932.
Courtesy Tampa-Hillsborough County Public Library System

LEFT: Construction is complete and a dedication ceremony is held for the federal veterans hospital and administration center on Seminole Point in 1933. The next year, the name was changed to Bay Pines and it remains a veterans hospital today. *Courtesy Archives of the St. Petersburg Times*

ABOVE: The bottom had fallen out of the St. Petersburg economy and people were looking for work. These were the Depression days of 1932 when this sign went up on the outskirts of town.
Courtesy Archives of the St. Petersburg Times

RIGHT: Front page of the *St. Petersburg Times*, March 6, 1933. *Courtesy Special Collections and Archives, Nelson Poynter Memorial Library, University of South Florida St. Petersburg*

BELOW: In the 1930s, money grew so short that scrip was issued by the St. Petersburg Citizens Emergency Committee. The *Times* was one of the companies that paid employees half in cash, half in scrip. The scrip could be used for groceries or at any store that advertised in the *Times*. Advertisers in turn paid their bills to the *Times* with scrip. *Courtesy Archives of the St. Petersburg Times*

ABOVE: The New Deal created all sorts of public work projects and the Tampa Bay area received its share. Here work continues on a Public Works Administration project next to Albert Whitted Airport in St. Petersburg, circa mid 1930s. *Courtesy Archives of the St. Petersburg Times*

TOP RIGHT: Another public works project involved laying water mains along a road in St. Petersburg, circa mid 1930s. *Courtesy Archives of the St. Petersburg Times*

BOTTOM RIGHT: Children at the Ritz Theatre in Tampa, shot from the stage to the rear of the building with its kitsch village décor, 1932. *Courtesy Tampa-Hillsborough County Public Library System*

BELOW: Postmaster General Jim Farley speaks at the dedication of the post office in Clearwater, 1933. *Courtesy Heritage Village Archives & Library*

ABOVE: People in Tampa wade through the flooded street in front of Hyman's Grocery at 1500 Grand Central Ave. on June 13, 1934. The city got almost eight inches of rain in a 24-hour period, the Times reported. *Courtesy Tampa-Hillsborough County Public Library System*

RIGHT: Matthew's Corner at 617 Franklin St. in Tampa, a newsstand with magazines, postcards and a soda fountain, 1935. *Courtesy Tampa-Hillsborough County Public Library System*

ABOVE: View of Straub Park, the Municipal Pier, Yacht basin, Spa Municipal Pool and the beach, looking east, in St. Petersburg, 1934. *Courtesy Tampa-Hillsborough County Public Library System*

LEFT: Strawberry Festival queen with her costumed court in Plant City, 1934. *Courtesy Tampa-Hillsborough County Public Library System*

BELOW: Sponge boats docked along Spring Boulevard in Tarpon Springs, circa 1934. *Courtesy Tampa-Hillsborough County Public Library System*

"Most of us undoubtedly would be intrigued by a glimpse into the future to see what life in the United States 100 years from now may be like.

The national resources committee reported on new industrial inventions which it feels may effect disturbing changes in employment, not only 100 years from now, but possibly within the next 20 years:

1. air-conditioning
2. trailers
3. plastics
4. prefabricated houses
5. television"

ABOVE: Uniformed women workers at Tampa Coca-Cola Bottling Co. at 612 Cass St. in Tampa, 1937. *Courtesy Tampa-Hillsborough County Public Library System*

RIGHT: Eight candidates for the Gasparilla court on the edge of a garden fountain in Tampa, 1936. *Courtesy Tampa-Hillsborough County Public Library System*

OPPOSITE: Chain-letter groups were popular in the 1930s, and this one gathered at a downtown St. Petersburg coffee shop on July 12, 1935. *Courtesy Archives of the St. Petersburg Times*

BELOW: A view of downtown Bradenton looking north, circa 1936. *Courtesy Tampa-Hillsborough County Public Library System*

ABOVE: Bishop Joseph P. Hurley, center in hat, poses with other clergy on the rectory steps at St. Paul Catholic Church on 12th Street N in St. Petersburg. St. Paul's first pastor, Father James Enright — on the top step just to the left of Bishop Hurley — had arrived in 1929 at age 27 and was responsible for opening the first Catholic school in Pinellas County in 1930. In 1931, he was instrumental in getting the Franciscan Sisters of Allegany, N.Y., to buy a hospital in St. Petersburg and open it as St. Anthony's. In March 1939, the parish dedicated its new church building, which is still in use today. *Courtesy St. Paul Catholic Church*

ABOVE: About 10,000 worshippers of many denominations attend a chilly Easter sunrise service near the Vinoy yacht basin in St. Petersburg on March 28, 1937. *Courtesy Archives of the St. Petersburg Times*

LEFT: In the 1920s and 1930s, some of St. Petersburg's most prominent residents were members of a resurgent Ku Klux Klan, which helped ensure that the city remained one of the most segregated communities in America. On July 19, 1937, more than 200 hooded klansmen marched through some of St. Petersburg's black neighborhoods. They vowed to retaliate if black voters turned out at the polls the next day, and they burned two crosses, one at the home of a man alleged to be the "Negro bolita king." Despite the threats, about 40 percent of the black registered voters cast ballots. *Courtesy Archives of the St. Petersburg Times.*

OPPOSITE TOP: A crowd gathers at the opening of St. Petersburg City Hall in late 1939. *Courtesy Archives of the St. Petersburg Times*

OPPOSITE BOTTOM LEFT: St. Petersburg Mayor John S. Smith and city manager A.F. Thomasson forgot the cares of the city long enough to enjoy a ride on a Ferris wheel at the Pinellas County Fair in Largo, 1937. *Courtesy Archives of the St. Petersburg Times*

OPPOSITE BOTTOM RIGHT: St. Petersburg City Hall, as it looked upon completion in late 1939, was one of several projects of the New Deal's Works Progress Administration. Other WPA projects were the Peter O. Knight Airport and Fort Homer Hesterly Armory in Tampa. *Courtesy Archives of the St. Petersburg Times*

The 1940s

When America entered World War II in December 1941, the Tampa Bay area was still trying to shake the Depression. But the war gave new life to the region's economy and led to a resurgence in the years that followed.

To be sure, the war brought anxiety, inconvenience and restrictions. Thousands of young men and women answered their country's call to duty, and many never came home. Blackouts were imposed. Essential food items were rationed. Gasoline was hard to get, new tires even harder.

Almost overnight, the streets of Clearwater, St. Petersburg and Tampa were filled with soldiers, sailors and pilots. Capitalizing on the region's mild climate and empty hotel rooms, the American military turned Tampa Bay into a major training center. Tens of thousands of recruits spent time here. Waves of young men in khaki and olive drab lived in the hotels, drilled in the parks, marched down the streets and relaxed at the restaurants, bars and beaches. In Tampa, three shipyards that employed thousands of workers turned out scores of ships and seagoing tugs.

When the war was over, many of those servicemen remembered the area. Some returned for vacations in the hotels that reverted to civilian use or the motels that sprang up along the beaches. Many tourists found their way to a new attraction – Weeki Wachee Springs in Hernando County. Other servicemen moved here. The influx of newcomers prompted a postwar housing boom that filled out half-built subdivisions and suburbs that grew around the cities.

Most military facilities changed hands or disappeared. Drew Field became Tampa International Airport, the Pinellas Army Air Base became St. Petersburg-Clearwater International and the Army Air Corps airport southwest of Brooksville became the Hernando County Airport. MacDill Field (now MacDill Air Force Base) remained and grew even more important as time passed.

The 1940s also marked a change of command and a change in editorial tone at the *Times*. When longtime editor W.L. Straub died in 1939, Paul Poynter's energetic son, Nelson, replaced him on the masthead. The young Poynter's first major crusade was a successful campaign to persuade local governments to refinance their staggering debts. His second, also successful, was a drive to improve low-cost housing for blacks by expanding Jordan Park. The *Times*, for many years a voice of Southern orthodoxy on questions of race, would gradually become a champion of equality. But the paper was quicker to endorse it on the editorial page than practice it in the newsroom.

LEFT: A crowd this large wasn't out of the ordinary for the friendly games that developed among ground crews as they waited for planes to come back to the Pinellas Army Air Base, now St. Petersburg-Clearwater International Airport. *Courtesy Archives of the St. Petersburg Times*

ABOVE: Shuffleboard Club members enjoy an afternoon of competition in St. Petersburg, 1940s. *Courtesy Archives of the St. Petersburg Times*

RIGHT: Labor Day parade in St. Petersburg, September 3, 1940. The Carpenters and Joiners Union No. 531 is leading this group. *Courtesy Archives of the St. Petersburg Times*

FAR RIGHT: A man holds the cross retrieved from the bayou during the annual Epiphany celebration in Tarpon Springs, 1941.
Courtesy Tampa-Hillsborough County Public Library System

LEFT: People crowd the Million Dollar Pier on a fine July day in 1941. The pier, which got its name from the million-dollar bond issue that paid for its construction in 1925-26, was for years a popular gathering spot and city landmark. The casino building at the end of the pier was demolished in 1967 and replaced in 1973.
Courtesy Archives of the St. Petersburg Times

BOTTOM LEFT: A busy intersection in St. Petersburg, early 1940s. *Courtesy Archives of the St. Petersburg Times*

BELOW: East Bay Drive, looking east at "Dutchman's Corner," Largo, 1941. *Courtesy Heritage Village Archives & Library*

"America Gives Its Answer to Japan's Day of Infamy, December 9, 1941

"With a promptness and unanimity that left no possible room for doubt, the United States yesterday answered with decisive action Japan's bloody, treacherous challenge.

We are in this thing now, all the way – and we are in to win. Our very survival depends upon complete victory....America, we know, will prove equal to the demands made upon her in this dark, momentous hour. We shall not, we cannot fail!"

ABOVE: A color guard made up of members of the United Spanish War Veterans, who had fought in the Spanish-American War, marches in a Labor Day parade in St. Petersburg in 1942.
Courtesy Archives of the St. Petersburg Times

RIGHT: Front page of the *St. Petersburg Times*, December 7, 1941. The headline, seven inches high, filled almost half the front page. The paper had no type that big. On a hunch, executive editor Tom Harris had the word "war" set in the biggest type available, then photographed, enlarged many times and set in a zinc engraving, just in case. Two weeks later, the Japanese attacked Pearl Harbor. *Courtesy Archives of the St. Petersburg Times*

OPPOSITE: World War II recruits arrive in St. Petersburg from one of the Army's reception areas, September 1940.
Courtesy Archives of the St. Petersburg Times

EXTRA St. Petersburg Times EXTRA

VOL. 58. NO. 136
COMPLETE ASSOCIATED PRESS UNITED PRESS AND INTERNATIONAL NEWS SERVICES
ST. PETERSBURG, FLORIDA, SUNDAY, DECEMBER 7, 1941
FIVE CENTS

JAPAN OFFICIALLY DECLARES
WAR
JAPS ATTACK HONOLULU, MANILA; F. D. R. ORDERS ARMY, FLEET INTO ACTION

TOKIO--Monday--(A.P.) -- Japanese imperial headquarters announced at 6 A.M. today that Japan had entered a state of war with the United States and Britain in the western Pacific as from dawn today.

WASHINGTON, Dec. 7.--(AP)--Japanese airplanes today attacked American defense bases at Hawaii and Manila, and President Roosevelt ordered the Army and Navy to carry out undisclosed orders prepared for the defense of the United States. Later it was reported it was all quiet at Manila.

The White House said that Japan had attacked America's vital outposts in the Pacific -- Hawaii and Manila -- at 3:20 P.M. (E.S.T.) and that so far as was known the attacks were still in progress.

Announcing the president's action for the protection of American territory, Presidential Secretary Stephen Early declared that so far as is known now the attacks were 'made wholly without warning -- when both nations were at peace -- and were delivered within an hour or so of the time that the Japanese ambassadors had gone to the state department to hand to the Secretary of State Japan's reply to the secretary's memorandum of the 26th.

Promptly, Navy officers said that long prepared counter measures against Japanese surprise attacks had been ordered into operation and were "working smoothly."

There was a disposition in some quarters here to wonder whether the attacks had not been ordered by the Japanese military authorities because they feared the president's direct negotiations with the emperor

HONOLULU--(UP)--Parachute troops were sighted off Harbor Point today.

might lead to an about-face in Japanese policy and the consequent loss of face by the present ruling factions in Japan.

The White House announced that heavy damage had been

inflicted in the Japanese attack on Hawaii and that there probably had been heavy loss of life.

The report of damage and casualties came to the White House from Rear Admiral C. C. Bloch, commanding the 14th naval district which embraces Hawaii.

The White House asserted, too, that Japan sent her bombers over the islands in dawn of early morning.

Asked about reports broadcast from Honolulu of a naval

engagement off Hawaii, presidential secretary Stephen Early said he could not confirm them.

A little later, the White House reported that an Army transport loaded with lumber had been torpedoed 1,300 miles west of San Francisco.

This is well east of Hawaii.

The first announcement did not say whether the ship was See WAR WITH JAPAN, Page 2, Col. 1

Turn to Page Four a Complete Pacific Map

98

ABOVE: Nelson Poynter, the son of *Times* publisher Paul Poynter, practically grew up in his father's newsrooms in St. Petersburg and Sullivan, Ind. He began buying his father's stock in the *Times* in 1935 and took the title of editor in 1939. He spent much of World War II in government positions in Washington and Hollywood. *Courtesy Special Collections and Archives, Nelson Poynter Memorial Library, University of South Florida St. Petersburg*

TOP RIGHT: Mrs. Roslyn Sobel, left, and Mrs. Robert Kramer inspect their war ration coupon books in St. Petersburg, circa 1942. *Courtesy Archives of the St. Petersburg Times*

RIGHT: The children of St. Paul Catholic School on 12th Street N in St. Petersburg show they are doing their part for the war effort by having a tin drive to collect metal for recycling, 1943. *Courtesy Archives of the St. Petersburg Times*

"Keep Mum, February 7, 1942

" **With German submarines operating off** the Atlantic coast, military and naval officials have re-emphasized the necessity for the American public refraining from repeating reports – true or untrue – that possibly might convey information of value to the enemy.

So, suggest the Army first corps headquarters, 'keep mum, chum.' "

ABOVE: "Not bad!" Bull's-eyes on a target are checked by Maj. Reed, left, Capt. Steward Robb and Lt. Richard Beaty, with Lt. Robert Venemon keeping score at the Pinellas Army Air Base, February 1943. *Courtesy Archives of the St. Petersburg Times*

TOP LEFT: GIs line up in front of the Tramor Cafeteria in St. Petersburg, 1942. During the war, St. Petersburg served as a basic training center. As a result, many hotels and cafeterias were taken over by the military. *Courtesy Archives of the St. Petersburg Times*

LEFT: Front page of the *St. Petersburg Times*, June 6, 1944. *Courtesy Special Collections and Archives, Nelson Poynter Memorial Library, University of South Florida St. Petersburg*

FAR LEFT: During the war, a road linking MacDill Field and Drew Field (now Tampa International Airport) was named in honor of Dale Mabry, a Florida native and veteran of World War I. Mabry was killed when the dirigible he was piloting crashed in Virginia in 1922. *Courtesy Hampton Dunn*

"Modern Crusaders Strike Blow for Freedom in France, June 7, 1944

"Generations to come will read about June 6, 1944.

It will rank with the landing of William of Normandy on English soil in 1066; it will rival the shot that was heard around the world at Lexington.

To us it was D-Day, the start of the greatest military operation in history. To France it is the day of liberation that she has awaited for four years. Even to the German people, there must come a sober thought at times that the cruel forces which have distorted their own lives are about to meet a reckoning.

Eisenhower's crusaders are carrying back the liberties Europe has lost."

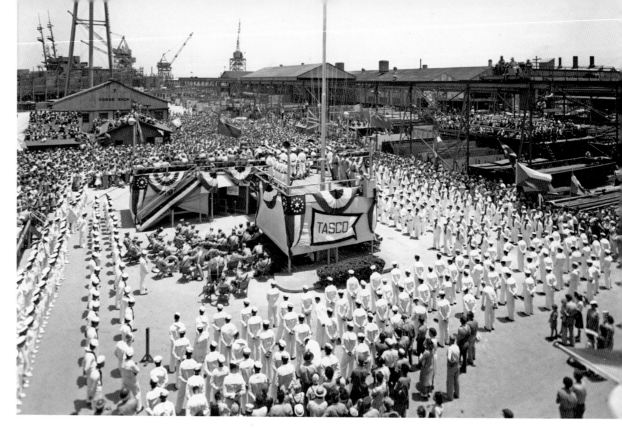

ABOVE: When the Tampa Shipbuilding Co. won an "E award" for its war production efforts in 1944, Gov. Spessard Holland joined the celebration. *Courtesy Tampa-Hillsborough County Public Library System*

BELOW: When Clearwater philanthropist Donald Roebling invented an amphibious tractor in the mid 1930s, he intended it to be a hurricane rescue vehicle. As World War II loomed, he adapted it for military operations at the request of the Marines and Navy. The vehicle, which Roebling dubbed the "Alligator," played a key role in the war. *Courtesy Archives of the St. Petersburg Times*

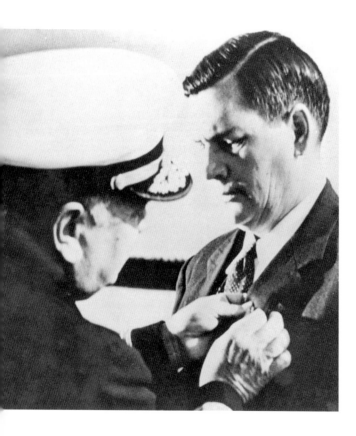

ABOVE: Roebling accepts a decoration from the military in the late 1940s for his invention, which he personally financed. He was a major benefactor of Morton Plant Hospital in Clearwater and other local causes. *Courtesy Archives of the St. Petersburg Times*

OPPOSITE: During World War II, the Pinellas Army Air Base (now St. Petersburg-Clearwater International Airport) was used by the Army as a military flight training base. *Courtesy Archives of the St. Petersburg Times*

A New World Begins, August 16, 1945

"It came fast. The war with Japan ended.

St. Petersburg returns to work after a holiday of celebration. Like in other parts of the country and in the world, the war's end signaled a spontaneous joy and enthusiasm here.

We have the tools, we have the manpower, we have the resources. The same will to peace that we exhibited to war will truly make the post-war era of our city, our state, our nation the greatest period in the history of the United States of America."

ABOVE: Front page of the *St. Petersburg Times*, August 14, 1945. The paper published three extra editions that day. *Courtesy Special Collections and Archives, Nelson Poynter Memorial Library, University of South Florida St. Petersburg*

TOP LEFT: Gasoline rationing was forgotten when a whistle blew to announce the surrender of Japan, August 1945. As the evening wore on, the celebration in St. Petersburg gained momentum. *Courtesy Archives of the St. Petersburg Times*

LEFT: Front page of the *St. Petersburg Times*, May 7, 1945. *Courtesy Special Collections and Archives, Nelson Poynter Memorial Library, University of South Florida St. Petersburg*

ABOVE: Delivery trucks opened wide to crowd in pedestrians on Central Avenue in St. Petersburg, celebrating Japan's surrender, August 1945. *Courtesy Archives of the St. Petersburg Times*

LEFT: Nearly four years of war separate the publication dates of these two *Times* editions exhibited by Helen Harrington, left, and Gloria Hummert on the steps of the administration building at the Coast Guard air station in St. Petersburg. Miss Hummert displays the *Times'* "war extra" heralding the start of the Pacific war following the infamous attack on Pearl Harbor, while Miss Harrington smiles at the banner headlines of Japan's surrender, August 1945. *Courtesy Archives of the St. Petersburg Times*

BELOW: Crowds line the street in St. Petersburg in celebration of the end of the war, 1945.
Courtesy Archives of the St. Petersburg Times

ABOVE: Students study electronics at the Don Thompson Vocational School in Tampa in 1948. In 2002, the theater at Blake High School was named for the former school. *Courtesy Pauline Larry Grant*

RIGHT: John Currier beats the throw to first baseman Clarence Merrill in a Kids and Kubs softball game in St. Petersburg in December 1942. The softball league was organized in 1930. *Courtesy Archives of the St. Petersburg Times*

BELOW: A crowd watches a Kids and Kubs game at Waterfront Park in this undated photo from the 1940s. In the background is the West Coast Inn at Third Avenue S and First Street. The hotel was demolished in 1967. The Hilton St. Petersburg Bayfront occupies the site today. *Courtesy Archives of the St. Petersburg Times*

ABOVE: For half a century, Silas Dent lived in a thatched cottage on Cabbage Key (known today as Tierra Verde). Dubbed "the happy hermit of Cabbage Key" by *Life* magazine in 1948, he lived off the land and sea. Every few weeks he rowed over to Pass-a-Grille, and at Christmas time he played Santa Claus for the beach community's children. "I haven't felt blue since 1912, and I forgot now what worried me," he told *Life*. He died in 1952 at the age of 76. *Courtesy Archives of the St. Petersburg Times*

TOP RIGHT: The Florida Fishing Tackle Co. does its bit in the war effort in 1945. Mrs. Julie Turner (left) and Mrs. Anna Stevens make fishing lures destined for the recreation of servicemen with the army of occupation in Germany. *Courtesy Archives of the St. Petersburg Times*

BELOW: Teachers Eula Fuller and Mary Polk pose with students during Class Day at Davis Elementary School in St. Petersburg in the 1940s. *Courtesy Heritage Village Archives & Library*

ABOVE: During the 1940s, publisher Paul Poynter gradually relinquished control of the *Times* to his son Nelson, who bought his father's remaining shares of Times Publishing Co. stock in 1947. In November 1950, Paul Poynter died. *Courtesy Special Collections and Archives, Nelson Poynter Memorial Library, University of South Florida St. Petersburg*

TOP RIGHT: The composing room of the *Times*, 1940s. In 1945, the workers who operated these linotype machines to typeset news and advertising copy went on strike over money and hours. The two-month strike was an awkward time for editor Nelson Poynter, who championed organized labor, except at his own paper. The *Times* broke the strike and strikes by *Times* pressmen in 1949 and 1952. *Courtesy Archives of the St. Petersburg Times*

RIGHT: A country-western band entertains shoppers at Jack Sheppard's Super Market at 1407 S Howard Ave. in Tampa in May 1946. *Courtesy Tampa-Hillsborough County Public Library System*

ABOVE: Officials break ground in November 1946 at the site of the proposed St. Petersburg Fair at 94th Avenue N between Fourth and Ninth streets. The officials, from left, are R.M. Williams, the fair's executive vice president; W.T. Baynard, its president; directors R.E. Wolfrath and Roy Bishop; W.D. Berry, vice president; Walter P. Fuller, public relations officer; and St. Petersburg Vice Mayor E.C. Robinson. The fair proved to be short-lived. *Courtesy Archives of the St. Petersburg Times*

LEFT: A section of Madeira Beach before the postwar development boom, circa 1946.
Courtesy Heritage Village Archives & Library

BOTTOM LEFT: St. Mary's Catholic Church on Fourth Street and Fifth Avenue S in St. Petersburg, 1940s.
Courtesy Archives of the St. Petersburg Times

BELOW: Cleaning up a train wreck in Mango, September of 1948. *Courtesy Tampa-Hillsborough County Public Library System*

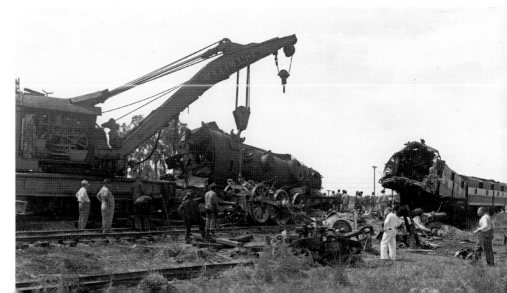

ABOVE: Past mayors of St. Petersburg and past presidents of the city's Chamber of Commerce, 1948. From left are Walter Tillinghast, chamber president in 1928; George Patterson, mayor 1943-47; C.C. Carr, former general manager of the *Times;* Roy S. Hanna, chamber president 1908; Al Lang, mayor 1916-19; and John Brown, mayor 1928-29. *Courtesy Archives of the St. Petersburg Times*

RIGHT: View of Franklin Street, Tampa, 1947.
Courtesy Archives of the St. Petersburg Times

BELOW: Virginia Hill stamps out fishing lures at Florida Fishing Tackle Co. at 2100 First Ave. S in St. Petersburg in 1946. The company was well-known for its Barracuda lures.
Courtesy Archives of the St. Petersburg Times

ABOVE: The Royal Theater on 22nd Street S, a movie house for black residents in St. Petersburg, awaits finishing touches in 1948. In the Jim Crow era, black people were banned from white theaters or required to watch from the balcony. The Royal closed when theaters integrated in the 1960s, then became the home of the Southside Boys' Club in the mid 1970s. *Courtesy Archives of the St. Petersburg Times*

RIGHT: Banana shipment being unloaded by stevedores and sorted by dock workers as it comes off the ship moored at the city dock in Tampa, 1947. *Courtesy Tampa-Hillsborough County Public Library System*

BELOW: More than 200 property owners fill the St. Petersburg City Council chambers in February 1948 to protest a proposal to expand the area where black residents can live. For years, St. Petersburg was one of the most segregated communities in America. By charter and custom, white city leaders sought to restrict African-Americans to a "city within a city." *Courtesy Archives of the St. Petersburg Times*

ABOVE: Nurses line the staircase next to the ancient Indian mounds just east of Mound Park Hospital (now Bayfront Medical Center) at Seventh Avenue S and Sixth Street in St. Petersburg, 1949. The mound of shells was demolished by the hospital's expansion in 1950. *Courtesy Archives of the St. Petersburg Times*

LEFT: St. Petersburg hired its first black officers in 1949, but they patrolled only in black neighborhoods. In this photo, Lt. C.G. Robinson, who supervised the new officers, demonstrates a judo hold to, from left, Sam Jones, Titus Robinson, Willie Seay and Louis Burrows. *Courtesy Archives of the St. Petersburg Times*

OPPOSITE TOP LEFT: By 1947, both police officials and outside investigators agree that the St. Petersburg city jail is deplorable. If a fire broke out, an American Legion committee says, "it could prove to be a death trap of terrific horrors." By the next year, the city had a new police station and a new jail.
Courtesy Archives of the St. Petersburg Times

OPPOSITE BOTTOM LEFT: Four female prisoners share a 10-by-6-foot cell in the city jail.
Courtesy Archives of the St. Petersburg Times

OPPOSITE RIGHT: The city jail, designed to hold 28 prisoners, sometimes had as many as 100, forcing many to sleep on the floor. *Courtesy Archives of the St. Petersburg Times*

ABOVE: L.D. Childs, who has been riding St. Petersburg's Big Bayou trolley line since 1914, bids farewell to the trolley and motorman E.F. Crawley on its final trip on January 11, 1948. As cars became more popular, streetcar passengers declined sharply. Tampa closed its last trolley line in 1946 and St. Petersburg in 1949. *Courtesy Archives of the St. Petersburg Times*

TOP RIGHT: Gov. Fuller Warren greets Betty Frankinson and other children at St. Petersburg Beach during Spans Across the Bay festivities in July 1949. The celebration heralded plans to build a bridge between south St. Petersburg and Manatee County and make Mullet Key a park (now called Fort De Soto). *Courtesy Archives of the St. Petersburg Times*

RIGHT: A Gasparilla parade makes its way down Tampa's Franklin Street in the late 1940s. Tampa's largest annual festival, Gasparilla began in the early 1900s and celebrates the legend of José Gaspar, a pirate whose mythical reign took place around the turn of the 18th century. *Courtesy Archives of the St. Petersburg Times*

ABOVE: Motorists await their turn to drive onto the Bee Line Ferry at the foot of Fourth Street S in St. Petersburg in 1949. Until the Sunshine Skyway opened in 1954, the main Pinellas-Manatee County connection was the ferry, which opened in 1926.
Courtesy Archives of the St. Petersburg Times

LEFT: The ferry makes its way across the seven miles between St. Petersburg's Pinellas Point and Manatee County in 1945.
Courtesy Archives of the St. Petersburg Times

The 1950s

As the 1950s began, Tampa was still struggling to clean up its image. Gang wars and political corruption gave the city nicknames like "Hell Hole of the Gulf Coast" and "Sin City of the South." The U.S. Senate's Kefauver Crime Investigating Committee brought unwelcome national publicity in 1950. And the murder of the city's reputed bolita kingpin five years later brought more.

The region's postwar growth spurt continued during the decade, which saw the coming of two key bridges, several institutions of higher learning and two developments that would transform America – air conditioning and television.

The Sunshine Skyway opened, and so did a second span of the Gandy Bridge. Work on the Howard Frankland Bridge started in 1957, with completion three years later. Construction of local links in the new interstate highway system began in Tampa. St. Petersburg celebrated when the last segment of U.S. 19 – between 22nd Avenue N and 18th Avenue S – was completed.

U.S. 19 became a growth corridor as newcomers began moving into the coastal counties north of Pinellas. In Pasco, builders and boosters touted the "$5,990" – a standard two-bedroom home on a small lot – in road signs and literature mailed up North. Within 15 years, the newcomers who clustered along 19 on the west side of Pasco, Hernando and Citrus outnumbered the long-timers on the east side.

Downtowns began to get some competition for shoppers – a trend that would intensify as people increasingly chose homes on or outside the rim of their cities. The suburban shopping center formula was pretty simple, according to historian Gary R. Mormino: Buy land along a busy road, dream up a snappy name, build a big parking lot and string together a bunch of little shops and at least one magnet (a grocery, drugstore or department store) in an L or U shape. The first suburban shopping centers in St. Petersburg were Tyrone Gardens and Central Plaza. In Tampa they were Northgate and Britton Plaza, and in Clearwater, Cleveland Plaza.

In Pinellas, some of the new residents worked in one of the defense industries that arrived in the mid 1950s. The so-called Big Four – Honeywell, ECI, General Electric and Sperry-Rand – brought fat payrolls, hundreds of well-educated engineers and, eventually, a number of subcontract suppliers.

Pinellas also became the seedbed of the modern Republican Party in Florida. It elected William C. Cramer to Congress in 1954, the first Republican congressman from Florida since Reconstruction. Cramer and two allies, Jack Insco and C.W. Bill Young, became so successful in getting Republicans elected to local offices that they became known as the "ICY machine" (ICY for Insco, Cramer and Young).

Gradually, two inventions began appearing in homes. Air conditioning, a novelty heretofore found mostly in department stores and movie theaters, spread to houses after the Carrier Corp. rolled out its low-cost window unit in 1951. The region's first television station, WSUN-Ch. 38, went on the air in 1953; WFLA-Ch. 8, two years later.

In 1954, Stetson Law School moved from DeLand to the former home of the Florida Military Academy (and before that the Roylat Hotel) in Gulfport. Tampa won the bidding for a new state university, and construction of the University of South Florida began near a former World War II airfield in 1957. St. Petersburg lost that project, but the next year Presbyterian Church leaders decided to put their proposed Florida Presbyterian College in the city. Thirteen years later, the college changed its name to honor benefactor Jack Eckerd, who had built a drugstore chain out of three small stores he acquired in Clearwater and Tampa in the early 1950s.

LEFT: Two lines of cars cross over the Sunshine Skyway bridge during opening ceremonies on Labor Day, 1954.
Courtesy Archives of the St. Petersburg Times

"We Take a Chance of All-Out War in the Hope of Lasting Peace, June 28, 1950

"**The way doctors prevent smallpox** epidemics is to give everyone a little case of controllable smallpox in the way of vaccination.

That, as we interpret it, is what President Truman, with almost unanimous support from the United Nations and our own Congress is attempting in the case of Korea.

In this action we are confident that the American people will back the Administration, even though dismayed by the threat of all-out war."

ABOVE: Segregated section of Al Lang Field in St. Petersburg, 1950. In the front row are S.W. Curtis Sr. and his wife, Gretchen Curtis. The crowd was enjoying a Marine Band matinee concert. Curtis was principal of Pinellas High School, which served black students in north Pinellas County, from 1927 to 1964. Curtis Fundamental Elementary School in Clearwater is named for his family. *Courtesy Archives of the St. Petersburg Times*

LEFT: Huge brick pile on St. Petersburg property at 49th Street and the Seaboard railroad tracks. The bricks covered an acre and formed the largest city stockpile. Some 250,000 were used for widening Ninth Street N and 1-million were used to widen other local streets. Nearly all these bricks were salvaged from Central Avenue. *Courtesy Archives of the St. Petersburg Times*

BELOW: View of Central Avenue looking east, St. Petersburg, circa 1950. *Courtesy Archives of the St. Petersburg Times*

LEFT: Campaigning for the post of department liaison officer to the City Council at police headquarters in St. Petersburg, June 1951. Candidates were Lt. E.C. "Bud" Hughes and A.C. Krupp, seen here passing out cigars to (from left) patrolmen Frank Bailey, Chris Odom, Bill Fishburne, Larry Tallman and Russ Barnes. *Courtesy Archives of the St. Petersburg Times*

LEFT: James Earl "Doc" Webb used countless gimmicks and low prices to promote his Webb's City, which covered several city blocks in St. Petersburg. Here he admires his Florida Poster Girls in 1951. *Courtesy Archives of the St. Petersburg Times*

FAR LEFT: Picketing mothers wage a "last ditch" battle for better drainage conditions in Larry's subdivision near Haines Road and 20th Street N in St. Petersburg. Marchers from left are Mrs. Robert Jackson, Mrs. B.C. Poston and Mrs. William Henzler. These women were the first shift of 30 subdivision mothers ready for the picket line. *Courtesy Archives of the St. Petersburg Times*

BELOW: St. Petersburg's new public library photographic charging machine was installed and put into use in August 1953. Mrs. V.C. Blackwell watches while library assistant Mrs. Jeanne Blakeslee places a book in the Recordak machine and photographs the borrower's card and date due. DeLyle Runge, library director, watches at right. *Courtesy Archives of the St. Petersburg Times*

ABOVE: Front page of the *St. Petersburg Times*, April 11, 1951. *Courtesy Special Collections and Archives, Nelson Poynter Memorial Library, University of South Florida St. Petersburg*

Forty Big Years, January 1, 1952

Along with the New Year, Pinellas County today celebrates its 40th birthday.

Pinellians have a good reason to celebrate. From literally nothing we have come to fourth among the State's counties in population....The *Times* is proud of the part it played in the creation and early days of Pinellas County. We hope that as Pinellas achieves new pinnacles we shall continue to be able to serve the County and the people well."

ABOVE: In August 1952, Capt. Eddie Rickenbacker, president of Eastern Air Lines, greets Hillsborough County Aviation Authority chairman J. Clifford MacDonald at the dedication of a new terminal at Tampa International Airport, which changed its name from Drew Field that year. Rickenbacker predicted in his speech that the airport would be outgrown and have to be expanded in three years. *Courtesy Archives of the St. Petersburg Times*

TOP RIGHT: The Maas Brothers float during the Gasparilla night parade in Tampa in 1954. *Courtesy Tampa-Hillsborough County Public Library System*

RIGHT: In March 1953, the worst fire in Pinellas County history swept through the Littlefield Nursing Home in Largo. The *Times* printed an extra edition later that day. Authorities ultimately determined that 33 patients died and 25 survived. The fire prompted reforms in state regulations. *Courtesy Special Collections and Archives, Nelson Poynter Memorial Library, University of South Florida St. Petersburg*

OPPOSITE: Three of the five members of the St. Petersburg Pelicans who played a minor-league all-star game at Al Lang Field in St. Petersburg in 1951. From left, Buddie Brockington, John Stevens and Clifford Jones. *Courtesy Archives of the St. Petersburg Times*

ABOVE: Middleton Senior High School girls basketball team in Tampa, 1954. *Courtesy Tampa-Hillsborough County Public Library System*

LEFT: Front page of the *St. Petersburg Times*, December 2, 1954. *Courtesy Special Collections and Archives, Nelson Poynter Memorial Library, University of South Florida St. Petersburg*

BELOW: Students dismissed from classes at St. Petersburg High School, circa 1954. *Courtesy Archives of the St. Petersburg Times*

ABOVE: When the Sunshine Skyway bridge opened in September 1954, the *Times* heralded it with a fat special edition. *Courtesy Special Collections and Archives, Nelson Poynter Memorial Library, University of South Florida St. Petersburg*

"A New Law, Make No Mistake about It. And It Appears to Be Final, May 18, 1954

"A major blow for man's freedom has been struck.

America can take pride in the patience and common sense of its white and black citizens that this major change is being made through our courts rather than through brawls and violence....Our highest court has recognized that legal validity to the concept of segregation does violence to the spirit – to the dignity – of those who are segregated..."

ABOVE: Little Sisters Glee Club members practice the theme song, *Blue Star,* for the TV series called *Medic.* The song was one in a group being presented at the 16th Street School auditorium in St. Petersburg during a summer enrichment program closing event. Pictured with the girls are E.A. Ponder, director, and Dorothy Johnson, accompanist. *Courtesy Archives of the St. Petersburg Times*

LEFT: Capt. Herman Humphries, receiving an alarm from the St. Petersburg fire headquarters switchboard operator, writes the location on his station's blackboard in October 1954. In the 1950s, when a citizen phoned in a fire, the operator relayed the information simultaneously by phone to all six fire stations and by radio to all trucks away from their stations. *Courtesy Archives of the St. Petersburg Times*

RIGHT: In the speakers' box at Al Lang Field, from left, are former Florida Gov. Fuller Warren; his wife, Barbara Manning Warren; U.S. Rep. James A. Haley of Sarasota; Mary Call Collins; and her husband, Democratic gubernatorial candidate LeRoy Collins. They were attending opening ceremonies for the Sunshine Skyway, September 1954. *Courtesy Archives of the St. Petersburg Times*

BELOW: Thousands attend the ceremonies for the Skyway at Al Lang Field, September 1954. *Courtesy Archives of the St. Petersburg Times*

ABOVE: The eight finalists in the Miss Sunshine Skyway bathing beauty contest at Anna Maria Island public beach, 1954. From left are Saundra Atkinson, Tampa; Sandra Kay Brokaw, Bradenton; Marsha Ann McFaddin, Bradenton; Patricia Norton, Tampa; Elaine Mickler, Tampa; the winner, Sonja Opp, St. Petersburg; Judy Shulse, St. Petersburg, and Donna Wentzel, Bradenton.
Courtesy Archives of the St. Petersburg Times

LEFT: In the 1950s, Weeki Wachee Springs in Hernando County was one of the nation's most popular tourist stops. The attraction received worldwide acclaim and has been used to film movies and TV shows. An $80,000 bathing beach and bath house opened in May 1956. *Courtesy Archives of the St. Petersburg Times*

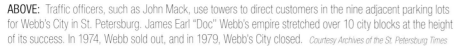

ABOVE: Traffic officers, such as John Mack, use towers to direct customers in the nine adjacent parking lots for Webb's City in St. Petersburg. James Earl "Doc" Webb's empire stretched over 10 city blocks at the height of its success. In 1974, Webb sold out, and in 1979, Webb's City closed. *Courtesy Archives of the St. Petersburg Times*

TOP RIGHT: One of the residents of Gator Lagoon at the Homosassa Springs State Wildlife Park, about 75 miles north of Tampa, nibbles on a sign, 1955. *Courtesy Archives of the St. Petersburg Times*

RIGHT: Bette Orsini and Phil Hicks kid around with the *Times'* new radio cars, June 1955. *Times* reporters would continue to use radios until the 1990s. In 1980, Orsini and Charles Stafford won the *Times* its second Pulitzer Prize for a series about the Church of Scientology. *Courtesy Archives of the St. Petersburg Times*

ABOVE: Jimmy Stewart, who plays a third baseman in the movie *Strategic Air Command,* shows off his throwing skills to St. Louis Cardinals manager Eddie Stanky during a break in filming at Al Lang Field in St. Petersburg, 1955. *Courtesy Archives of the St. Petersburg Times*

TOP LEFT: Leon Cazin, Fiesta president, with (from left) Norma Lopez, 1954 queen; Norma Dolores Lopez, 1952 queen; and Marie Jo-Ann Mirabelle, 1955 queen, planning the 29th edition of Ybor City's Latin American Fiesta, March 17-24, 1956. *Courtesy Archives of the St. Petersburg Times*

LEFT: Visiting during a lull in filming are (from left) Stewart, director Anthony Mann (in stands), August Busch Jr., owner of the St. Louis Cardinals, June Allyson, Cardinals manager Eddie Stanky and Jay C. Flippen, a member of the movie's cast, 1955. *Courtesy Archives of the St. Petersburg Times*

ABOVE: The August 8, 1956, edition of the *Times* said of Elvis Presley, seen here in a photo by *Times* photographer Bob Moreland, "He hit St. Petersburg with the effect of a small H-bomb."
Courtesy Archives of the St. Petersburg Times

RIGHT: Before playing in St. Petersburg, Presley plays two shows at Tampa's Fort Homer Hesterly Armory on August 5, 1956. Tickets were $1.50 for general admission; $2 for reserved seats.
Courtesy Archives of the St. Petersburg Times

OPPOSITE TOP: Longtime friends Mrs. C.H. Hobe, left, of St. Petersburg and Mrs. E.G. Heideman of Tampa attend the festivities celebrating the opening of a second span of the Gandy Bridge in Tampa in April 1956. *Courtesy Archives of the St. Petersburg Times*

OPPOSITE BOTTOM: Hours before the show, hundreds of Presley's fans crowd the sidewalks outside the Florida Theater in St. Petersburg on August 7, 1956. About 6,500 people packed into the theater for the show. *Courtesy Archives of the St. Petersburg Times*

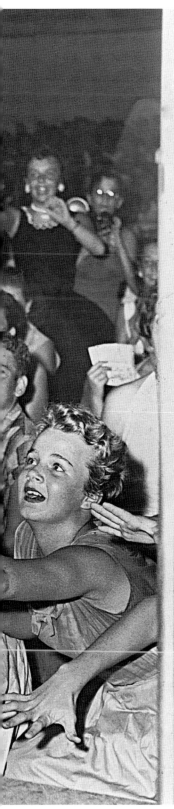

Bridges and the Tampa Bay Community, June 3, 1953

"Bridges constructed by modern methods should endure at least a half-century. That means anything built now should be serviceable well beyond the year 2000. And that means that we need to think about what the Tampa Bay metropolitan area is going to be like in the year 2000."

ABOVE: Workmen pour concrete in January 1959 for seawalls on the Tampa side of what would become known as the Howard Frankland Bridge across Tampa Bay. W. Howard Frankland, a prominent Tampa merchant, banker and member of the old state Road Board, had proposed in 1953 that a third bridge be built over the bay. Construction started in June 1957. *Courtesy Archives of the St. Petersburg Times*

ABOVE: The bridge's deck rests on concrete girders supported on concrete piers and steel piles, 1958. *Courtesy Archives of the St. Petersburg Times*

LEFT: Construction workers move from point to point on the emerging bridge on cables suspended from a crane, July 1958. The bridge was completed in August 1959 at a cost of $6.5-million. Not long after it opened in 1960, a state highway official called it a "death trap." Head-on collisions became so numerous that a raised concrete wall divider had to be installed. A second span was opened alongside the original in 1991. *Courtesy Archives of the St. Petersburg Times*

FAR LEFT: Workmen smooth one of the 348 spans of reinforced concrete deck slab that make up the bridge, 1959. The overall length of the bridge, when completed, will be 15,872 feet. *Courtesy Archives of the St. Petersburg Times*

LEFT: Nelson Poynter marks up an edition of the *St. Petersburg Times*, 1959. *Courtesy Special Collections and Archives, Nelson Poynter Memorial Library, University of South Florida St. Petersburg*

FAR LEFT: Keith Amos, Melvin Hutchinson and Dickie Ludwell show their skills in a three-legged race in July 1959. Some 600 youngsters were involved with the St. Petersburg City Recreation Department's summer enrichment program. *Courtesy Archives of the St. Petersburg Times*

OPPOSITE: Boats surround the Gasparilla ship as it heads toward the Platt Street Bridge in Hillsborough River. Photo taken from Tampa General Hospital, 1959. *Courtesy Tampa-Hillsborough County Public Library System*

BELOW: Work continues on the library, left, and the administration building at the University of South Florida northeast of Tampa, December 1959. The university's first president, John S. Allen, helped Gov. LeRoy Collins break ground for the school in September 1957. On September 26, 1960, nearly 2,000 students began classes in five buildings. *Courtesy Archives of the St. Petersburg Times*

LEFT: On June 5, 1958, eight young African-Americans leave the segregated Spa Beach in St. Petersburg. They spent about 40 minutes using the beach and locker rooms, but city officials immediately closed the beach in defiance of a federal court order that allowed black people to use the pool and beach. Seven months later, the City Council voted 4-3 to open the facility to all. *Courtesy Archives of the St. Petersburg Times*

The 1960s

A decade of breakthroughs in civil rights began in March 1960, when young black demonstrators were refused service at lunch counters in St. Petersburg and Tampa. Within a year, they had achieved their goal. As time passed, other barriers fell one by one – movie theaters, restrooms, restaurants, hospitals, public swimming pools and golf courses.

St. Petersburg hotels began admitting black guests after the New York Yankees forsook their longtime spring training home in the city for Fort Lauderdale in 1961. The team had come under fire from Northern newspapers because its black players had to find housing in private homes.

St. Petersburg was tested again in 1968, when the city's garbage workers – almost all of them black – went on strike. The next four months saw marches, picketing at City Council members' homes and three days of rioting. The strikers never got the raise they sought, but the white business establishment began taking hesitant steps toward ending generations of inequality and injustice at City Hall and in the business community. The next year, voters sent the council its first black member – C. Bette Wimbish.

In 1962 and 1963, hard freezes dealt crippling blows to the citrus industry in Tampa Bay. The John S. Taylor Packing Plant, one of Largo's largest employers, closed after 60 years. All over the region, grove land gave way to housing and shops. Much of the new housing was in apartments. Mandalay Shores, the largest apartment complex on Florida's west coast, opened in Clearwater Beach. By 1970, six of every 10 new housing units in St. Petersburg were apartments.

Fed up with their salaries and meager state spending on schools, 40 to 50 percent of Florida's 58,000 teachers went on strike in 1968. Some stayed out a few days, some as long as three months. Hillsborough County's teachers were led by Bob Martinez, a future Tampa mayor and governor. The teachers ultimately won higher salaries, more dollars for schools and the right to bargain collectively (while giving up the right to strike). But public opinion ran against them in some school districts, and bitter feelings lingered for years.

St. Petersburg got a Museum of Fine Arts, a federal office building, a new main library, a new municipal marina and an entertainment complex called the Bayfront Center. But the downtown core deteriorated. Plans for a two-block-long business and hotel complex called Bayfront Plaza fizzled, and image-conscious officials pulled out the city's green benches, which they feared had become a symbol of a listless, elderly town. (Typical of the national publicity was one magazine's description: "The old people sit, passengers in a motionless streetcar without destination.")

The Clearwater Pass Bridge opened, linking Clearwater Beach to Sand Key and the beaches below it. The Pinellas Bayway, a dredge-and-fill project and toll road that linked south St. Petersburg to St. Petersburg Beach and spawned countless condominiums, was pushed through despite its damage to the environment. But a proposed Clearwater-to-St. Petersburg toll road died in the Legislature.

In Tampa, a hospitality center at the Anheuser-Busch Brewery turned into a major tourist attraction. The trees and pasture land in West Shore gave way to office towers, hotels and financial institutions. Tampa Stadium was built for the University of Tampa football team. The stadium endured; the team didn't.

Retirees flocked to west Pasco in the 1960s to buy bargain houses in new subdivisions. As the county's population more than doubled, its median age increased from 38.5 to 53.4. A similar explosion began in west Hernando in 1967, when the Deltona Corp. opened Spring Hill, a community that quickly dwarfed Brooksville and began transforming the county's politics, economy and social character.

The *Times* had reached 100,000 in average daily circulation in 1959, but Nelson Poynter was never satisfied. When told by a lieutenant that an idea was impossible or impractical, he would whip out a dime (the price of the paper) and declare, "I'm a reader; don't tell me you can't do it." After winning its first Pulitzer Prize in 1964, the paper began calling itself "Florida's Best Newspaper" on the Page 1 nameplate. It was another way for Poynter to challenge the staff.

LEFT: Onlookers peer in as Freedom Riders eat lunch at the Greyhound Bus Station in St. Petersburg in June 1961. Received peacefully here, elsewhere the Freedom Riders were attacked with clubs and rocks, beaten, jailed and often in fear for their lives. Seated at the table are Francis Randall and Ralph Diamond. *Courtesy Archives of the St. Petersburg Times*

"A New University Becomes a Reality, September 26, 1960

"**A set of buildings, a** faculty and a curriculum become a university today. The catalyst: 1,500 freshmen who'll take up pad and pencil to put the learning operation under way at the University of South Florida (USF).

....Addresses will be delivered by Gov. LeRoy Collins and USF president Dr. John S. Allen. Part of the dedication program will be visitor tours of campus buildings before official opening of classes at 11 a.m."

ABOVE: Children in a summer enrichment program learn how slugs of type are made at the *Times*, July 1960. *Courtesy Archives of the St. Petersburg Times*

TOP LEFT: C. Bette Wimbish is surrounded by supporters as she sits at a table in her campaign headquarters, April 1960. Mrs. Wimbish sought the Democratic nomination for a seat on the Pinellas School Board. She did not win that election, but in 1969 she became the first black person elected to the St. Petersburg City Council. *Courtesy Archives of the St. Petersburg Times*

LEFT: The Major League Old Timers Baseball Game parade on Central Avenue in St. Petersburg, February 1961. *Courtesy Archives of the St. Petersburg Times*

LEFT: The St. Petersburg NAACP sponsored this movement in cooperation with the Congress of Racial Equality to boycott local businesses that refused to serve African-Americans, December 1960. Even before lunch counters were desegregated, the *Times* joined Gov. LeRoy Collins in asserting that it was "morally wrong" to deny service to blacks. *Courtesy Archives of the St. Petersburg Times*

BELOW: On Jan. 3, 1961, Dr. Ralph Wimbish, president of the St. Petersburg branch of the NAACP, is served at the Maas Brothers department store lunch counter. That same day, 14 other lunch counters around St. Petersburg also quietly integrated, ending weeks of sit-ins and picketing. Dr. Wimbish spent much of his life campaigning against racial injustice and saw the integration of St. Petersburg's lunch counters, theaters, public restrooms, swimming areas, junior college and public hospital before he died in 1967 of a heart attack at the age of 45. *Courtesy Archives of the St. Petersburg Times*

BOTTOM LEFT: Craig Gree, son of Mr. and Mrs. Todd Gree, takes gleeful command of a parked cruiser as part of a group of 120 who visited St. Petersburg Police headquarters on July 11, 1961. They were among 592 children enrolled in a summer enrichment program. *Courtesy Archives of the St. Petersburg Times*

ABOVE: Front page of the *St. Petersburg Times*, December 13, 1962. The page was printed in blue ink during a record cold spell in the Tampa Bay area. *Courtesy Archives of the St. Petersburg Times*

TOP LEFT: A crowd gathers at St. Petersburg-Clearwater International Airport for the inaugural flight of National Airlines' non-stop service to New York, November 8, 1960.
Courtesy Archives of the St. Petersburg Times

LEFT: A group of young African-Americans and white people march and chant on June 20, 1963, as they picket two downtown Tampa theaters demanding that they integrate. *Courtesy Archives of the St. Petersburg Times*

OPPOSITE: Joe DiMaggio and his former wife, film star Marilyn Monroe, relax at the Tides Hotel and Bath Club Resort on North Redington Beach in 1961. When the club opened in 1936, it was south Pinellas County's only private club. The resort was demolished in 1996. *Courtesy Archives of the St. Petersburg Times*

ABOVE: This St. Petersburg motorist got so excited at the prospect of getting gas for 19.9 cents a gallon at Webb's City Gas Station that she forgot to look at her gas gauge. Photo circa 1961.
Courtesy Archives of the St. Petersburg Times

TOP RIGHT: By 1963, Busch Gardens in Tampa was drawing 1-million visitors a year. The attraction, which opened to the public on June 1, 1959, featured a tour of the beer brewery, a Hospitality House, an amphitheater for animal shows, herds of buffalo, zebra, deer, ostrich and retired Clydesdales, and Dwarf Village. Construction on the Old Swiss House restaurant began in December 1963. *Courtesy Archives of the St. Petersburg Times*

RIGHT: The *José Gasparilla*, a fully rigged pirate ship commissioned in 1954 by Ye Mystic Krewe, is accompanied by an armada of pleasure craft as it sails through the open jaws of Tampa's gateway bridges on February 10, 1963, for the invasion and parade that are part of the annual Gasparilla Carnival. The name comes from a fictional pirate named José Gaspar. *Courtesy Archives of the St. Petersburg Times*

ABOVE: Guy Lombardo and his orchestra perform at the Fort De Soto Park dedication ceremony on May 11, 1963. In the early 1960s, Lombardo was part owner of the $5-million Port-o-Call vacation resort on Tierra Verde. *Courtesy Archives of the St. Petersburg Times*

LEFT: The Rev. A. Leon Lowry waits outside the White House in the early 1960s for an appointment with President John F. Kennedy. The Rev. Lowry was one of Tampa's most influential civil rights activists, president of the Florida NAACP and, in 1976, became the first African-American elected to the Hillsborough County School Board, where he served four terms. He died of congestive heart failure in August 2005 at age 92. *Courtesy Archives of the St. Petersburg Times*

FAR LEFT: Helping St. Petersburg Mayor Herman Goldner to the dance floor during a ball at the Coliseum in April 1963 are Dana Mansur, left, and Nancy Allen. *Courtesy Archives of the St. Petersburg Times*

"He Shall Not Have Died in Vain," November 23, 1963

"Disbelief. Shock. Anguish. Outrage – a thundering, towering outrage, mingled with shame, guilt and remorse.

Is there a citizen of the United States worthy of the name who did not feel these emotions yesterday afternoon?

John Fitzgerald Kennedy, 35th President of the United States, only last Monday – Monday of this week – smilingly greeting his Suncoast admirers at Al Lopez Field, freely, casually pressing through crowds, warmly shaking hands with everyone who could reach him.

....The assassination of President Kennedy gives the United States a new goal. It must now prove to the world that democracy can work without eruptions of violence, that men can live in both freedom and justice."

ABOVE: President John F. Kennedy rides in a convertible as he leaves the tarmac at MacDill Air Force Base in Tampa on November 18, 1963, only four days before his assassination in Dallas, Texas. *Courtesy Archives of the St. Petersburg Times*

RIGHT: Front page of the *St. Petersburg Times*, November 23, 1963. *Courtesy Special Collections and Archives, Nelson Poynter Memorial Library, University of South Florida St. Petersburg*

OPPOSITE: President John F. Kennedy's motorcade travels down Lafayette Street where it splits off from Grand Central Avenue in Tampa. Kennedy made three speeches during his visit to the city on that Monday in November. Because the motorcade had traveled about 5 miles on Grand Central, the Tampa City Council voted unanimously in 1964 to rename it Kennedy Boulevard. *Courtesy Archives of the St. Petersburg Times*

RIGHT: This group of water skiing enthusiasts skied 1,200 miles from St. Petersburg to the World's Fair in New York City in July 1964. The trip was sponsored by the St. Petersburg Chamber of Commerce. At left, front to back, are Eric Bagg, Sonny Wagner and Dave Outen. In the next row are Michael Outen, Bobbi Kuykendall and Carol Patton. At right are Jim Gray, director of the chamber's city news bureau, and Paula Young. *Courtesy Archives of the St. Petersburg Times*

BELOW: Up the Wadmalaw River in South Carolina, skiers Randy Rabe, left, and Dave Dretten reach out for refreshments as they ski to New York. *Courtesy Archives of the St. Petersburg Times*

ABOVE: In the 1960s, *Times* reporter Sam Adams, center, with his wife, Eleanor, and reporter Jim Lewis and his wife, was the only black journalist covering the civil rights movement for a mainstream paper in the South. In 1964, he wrote a series called "Highways to Hope" about the experiences he and his wife had as they traveled the South testing compliance with the new Civil Rights Act. *Courtesy Archives of the St. Petersburg Times*

Fitting Examples, July 3, 1964

"**The civil rights bill of** 1964 is now law. As it became law the nation was given two examples of how it can begin to meet the adjustments required. One example came from a southern President seeking support and compliance for what is morally and legally right. With such examples to follow, America can reach its goal of liberty and justice for all. Yesterday, we took a great step along the way."

ABOVE: Peggy Mitchell Peterman was hired by the paper in 1965 to write for its "Negro news page" – a page of news and notes about the black community that circulated only in African-American neighborhoods. She helped persuade *Times* editors to abolish the page in 1967, arguing that it helped perpetuate segregation. Peterman spent 31 years on the staff as a reporter, columnist and editorial writer. She retired from the paper in 1996 and died on August 19, 2004, at the age of 67. *Courtesy Archives of the St. Petersburg Times*

LEFT: Joe Waller (center in dark sweater and dark glasses) and his supporters walk down Central Avenue on December 30, 1966, after ripping down a mural in St. Petersburg's City Hall that depicted racially caricatured black people entertaining white picnickers at a beach. A *Times* editorial called the protesters "extremists" and their behavior "hoodlumism." In the decades since, Waller changed his name to Omali Yeshitela and became leader in the National People's Democratic Uhuru Movement. *Courtesy Archives of the St. Petersburg Times*

ABOVE: Beautification project, Maderia Beach, circa 1965. *Courtesy Heritage Village Archives & Library*

BELOW: Giant cranes lower hydros in the water for the second heat of the $25,000 Suncoast Cup Regatta at Courtney Campbell Parkway in Tampa, June 13, 1966. *Courtesy Archives of the St. Petersburg Times*

ABOVE: Striking St. Petersburg sanitation employees march east on Third Avenue S to Fifth Street and north to City Hall, July 1965. The police kept most of the men from entering City Hall.
Courtesy Archives of the St. Petersburg Times

BELOW: Miss Tarpon Springs first runner-up Rozanne Sarris (on couch) prepares to make a call as her friend Helen Katsuris cautions her that beginning in a few days she must dial all seven digits. The entire Tarpon Springs prefix "937" must be dialed, according to an announcement by Dick Houston, the commercial manager of General Telephone's office in New Port Richey and Tarpon Springs. *Courtesy Archives of the St. Petersburg Times*

What About Tomorrow?
May 6, 1964

"Spirits have been soaring at the *Times* since mid-afternoon Monday when a telegram arrived announcing that this newspaper had won the 1964 Pulitzer Gold Medal for public service.

....The timing of the announcement, arriving at the climax of important county and state elections, should help the staff keep its feet on solid ground. It reminds us that our clients – our readers – aren't awed by honors based on last year's big story. Like the skeptical political supporter, they ask: 'What have you done for me today? And what about tomorrow?'

It's those todays and tomorrows toward which a newspaper deserving its honors must work."

BOVE: Nelson Poynter (on desk) and (from left) executive editor Don Baldwin, general manager Tom Harris and managing editor Cortland nderson get word that the *St. Petersburg Times* has won its first Pulitzer Prize on May 4, 1964. The paper was honored for its stories on irregulari- es at the Florida Turnpike Authority. *Courtesy Special Collections and Archives, Nelson Poynter Memorial Library, University of South Florida St. Petersburg*

ELOW: A 1967 aerial view of Spa Beach and the downtown St. Petersburg waterfront. From left, in the background are the Bayfront Center, arlton Towers and the new Federal Building. *Courtesy Archives of the St. Petersburg Times*

ABOVE: Sandy Koufax of the Los Angeles Dodgers pitches against the New York Mets during a spring training game at Al Lang Field in St. Petersburg in March 1964. *Courtesy Archives of the St. Petersburg Times*

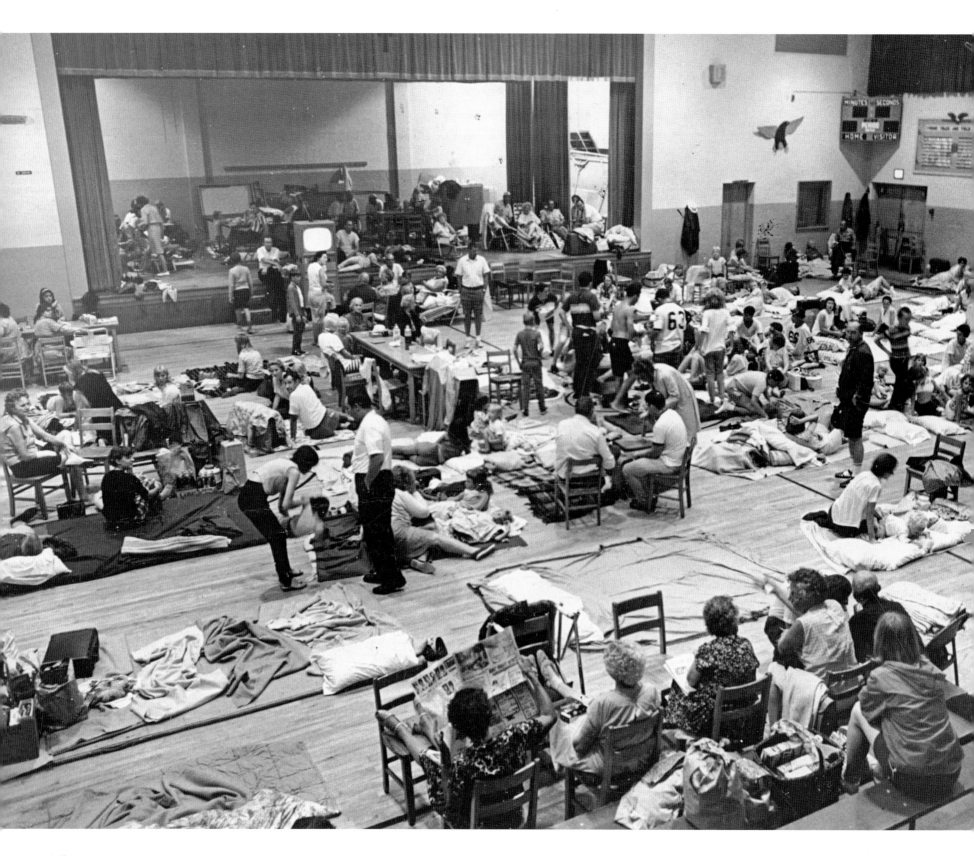

It's Still the Answer, April 5, 1968

"**The long road from Montgomery** was ended for Dr. Martin Luther King by an assassin's bullet in Memphis.

Along the way, Dr. King helped bring his nation to some of its finest hours.

His violent death was one of its darkest.

The danger now is that the brutal murder of Dr. King will strengthen those who preach both racism and violence.

But the great majority of Americans of all races should know that the answer of Gandhi and Martin Luther King was the right one.

It is the truth that prevails even after assassins fire their futile bullets."

ABOVE: National Guardsmen, on patrol, walk past a smashed storefront on June 12, 1967, during a second night of rioting in Tampa after Martin Chambers, an unarmed black teenager, was shot in the back by white Patrolman James Calvert, who was chasing three robbery suspects. Chambers' death sparked three nights of rioting. *Courtesy Archives of the St. Petersburg Times*

TOP LEFT: Front page of the *St. Petersburg Times*, April 5, 1968. *Courtesy Special Collections and Archives, Nelson Poynter Memorial Library, University of South Florida St. Petersburg*

LEFT: A National Guardsman frisks suspects for weapons during three nights of rioting in Tampa. Overall, 500 Florida National Guardsmen, more than 200 Florida Highway Patrol troopers and 250 local law enforcement officers are called to assist during the disturbances. *Courtesy Archives of the St. Petersburg Times*

FAR LEFT: Residents who evacuated their homes as Hurricane Alma moved through the eastern Gulf of Mexico in June 1966 crowd the gymnasium at Tyrone Junior High School in St. Petersburg. The hurricane eventually came ashore in the Florida Panhandle. *Courtesy Archives of the St. Petersburg Times*

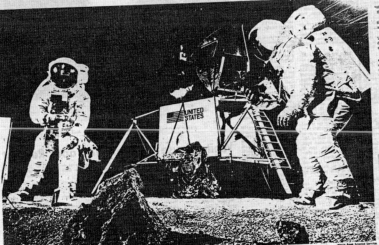

What a Piece of Work, July 22, 1969

"**Apollo 11 is coming home.** But the soul of mankind never will come back – not completely anyway.

Man approaches this new age with a greater understanding than he has ever known. Wars have been the only turnings of history in which broad masses have been involved, until now.

Because the attitudes of men are decisive in plotting the course of history, so much is implied in the peaceful, adventurous spirit of moonflight. This is the meaning of Apollo 11."

ABOVE: A judge swears in C. Bette Wimbish, widow of NAACP leader Ralph Wimbish, as the first African-American elected to the St. Petersburg City Council in March 1969. She served with Barbara Gammon, making it also the first time two women were on the council at the same time. *Courtesy Archives of the St. Petersburg Times*

LEFT: Front page of the *St. Petersburg Times*, July 21, 1969. *Courtesy Special Collections and Archives, Nelson Poynter Memorial Library, University of South Florida St. Petersburg*

The 1970s

The civil rights gains of the 1960s reached the schools of Pinellas and Hillsborough counties in the fall of 1971. Under pressure from black plaintiffs and the U.S. Supreme Court, both school districts implemented countywide desegregation plans. The Pinellas plan was one of the most sweeping in the country.

In local politics, it was a decade of firsts. James Sanderlin, the lawyer who spearheaded the Pinellas desegregation lawsuit, became the first black person elected to countywide office in Pinellas. He won a county judgeship in 1972. Leon Lowry, a minister and civil rights leader in Tampa, was the first in Hillsborough; he was elected to the School Board in 1976. Catherine Barja became the first woman elected to the Tampa City Council (1971), Betty Castor the first at the Hillsborough County Commission (1972) and Jeanne Malchon the first at the Pinellas commission (1976). Corinne Freeman became the first woman elected mayor in St. Petersburg in 1977. (Tampa elected its first woman mayor, Sandy Freedman, in 1986.)

The decade saw the opening of Tampa International Airport's new landside/airside terminal complex, and second spans for the Sunshine Skyway and Gandy bridges. The first segment of the Crosstown Expressway in Tampa opened, but voters rejected a second attempt to build a toll road linking south Pinellas to north Pinellas and Pasco.

There were disasters – a huge oil spill when a tanker ran aground in Tampa Bay in 1970 and a tornado that struck a Pinellas elementary school in 1979, killing three youngsters. There were beginnings – regional malls like Tyrone Square in St. Petersburg, Clearwater and Countryside in Clearwater and University Square in Tampa (which got the first regional mall, WestShore Plaza in 1967). And there was an ending. Webb's City, the gim-micky retailer that once had 77 stores covering several city blocks in St. Petersburg, closed in 1979. There was even snow. On January 19, 1977, a storm left a half-inch of the white stuff on the ground.

The Church of Scientology, an organization founded by science fiction author L. Ron Hubbard, bought Clearwater's Fort Harrison Hotel and began bringing in staff and students. For weeks, however, it misled the city about its identity. That set the tone for years of dirty tricks by the church as it battled its perceived enemies at City Hall, the Police Department, the *Times* and *Clearwater Sun*.

For years, the governments of St. Petersburg and Pinellas – which got most of their water from well fields in Hillsborough and Pasco – had feuded with those neighbors as water demand soared amid population gains and prolonged droughts. In the mid 1970s, the governments finally formed a regional water management authority designed to foster cooperation.

As fighting over water declined, there was a new reason to feud: baseball. Pinellas and Hillsborough spent 15 acrimonious years in pursuit of a team. There was no such competition over football, however. The National Football League awarded Tampa a franchise in 1974, and two years later the Tampa Bay Buccaneers began play.

The *Times* was growing as rapidly as the region it served, and in 1971 it passed the *Tampa Tribune* to become Florida's second largest newspaper (behind the *Miami Herald*). A year later, Eugene Patterson, a Pulitzer Prize winner at the *Atlanta Constitution* in 1967, became Poynter's top deputy.

Poynter always thought ahead. He feared that, after his death, the paper his family had owned since 1912 might end up in a chain run by corporate outsiders who valued big profits over readers. So he created a nonprofit school for journalists, left most of the *Times'* stock to it and designated a successor – Patterson – to run both the school and the paper. He even left instructions on how his obituary should be handled. When he died in 1978, the transition appeared to be seamless.

LEFT: St. Petersburg's new Pier, an inverted pyramid, sports a winter carnival atmosphere for its official opening in January 1973.
Courtesy Archives of the St. Petersburg Times

153

ABOVE: Motorists approaching Tampa's new $85-million airside-landside terminal at Tampa International Airport often get a shock seeing jets crossing the airport's entrance road on this elevated taxiway. Construction on the airport was completed in October 1970. *Courtesy Archives of the St. Petersburg Times*

TOP LEFT: Owen Weld of New Port Richey keeps a close eye on the race at the opening of the 1978 season at Florida Downs and Turf Club (Tampa Bay Downs). *Courtesy Archives of the St. Petersburg Times*

LEFT: Workmen go about the task of building a highway in St. Petersburg, April 1970. The support structure for a segment of I-275 near Roosevelt Boulevard is nearly complete. *Courtesy Archives of the St. Petersburg Times*

BELOW: Sweeping desegregation of Pinellas County's schools began in the fall of 1971. At some schools, there were protests, fights and arrests. On October 12, Betty Newby seeks help as her daughter Audrey is arrested outside Dixie Hollins High School. *Courtesy Archives of the St. Petersburg Times*

Footholds for the Future, February 22, 1972

"Today, as President Nixon visits China, much of the world saw him depart and arrive, and is following events closely as the President and his hosts meet, dine, converse and offer congenial toasts.

Let's establish diplomatic recognition, and that done, let the two nations expand trade agreements, cultural exchanges and tourism, the small but necessary footholds for the future."

ABOVE: Florida Presbyterian College gets a new name and a new sign as Dr. Billy Wireman, college president, makes it official in June 1971. Jack M. Eckerd, a college trustee and chairman of the board of the Jack Eckerd Corp., became the school's major benefactor with a gift of $10-million. *Courtesy Archives of the St. Petersburg Times*

ABOVE: Mermaids at Weeki Wachee Springs conduct a "smash trash" drive covering the six miles of State Road 50 from the attraction to the Gulf of Mexico. The mermaids are Carol Bates, at the wheel, with Nibsie Towne and April Moffitt doing the loading in May 1971. They were removing trash and rubbish scattered along the right-of-way. *Courtesy Archives of the St. Petersburg Times*

RIGHT: Jacques Cousteau (left) visits Crystal River to film manatees for an underwater TV series in 1971. The Miami Seaquarium loaned the manatee that is wrapped in wet blankets in the truck. *Courtesy Archives of the St. Petersburg Times*

ABOVE: Publix Super Markets won top prize in the commercial category during the Chasco Fiesta's golden anniversary parade in New Port Richey in 1972. The parade kicked off the weeklong fiesta, the area's annual salute to its Calusa Indian heritage. *Courtesy Archives of the St. Petersburg Times*

BELOW: A resident sits at a bus stop on Beach Boulevard after Hurricane Agnes caused severe flooding and high winds in Pinellas County in 1972. The storm came ashore in the Florida Panhandle on June 19, crossed the Southeast and emerged in the Atlantic Ocean off North Carolina before making landfall again near New York City on June 22. Agnes' severe flooding and thunderstorms caused 122 deaths and was responsible for $2.1-billion in damage in the United States. *Courtesy Archives of the St. Petersburg Times*

ABOVE: Servando Lopez, 76, was one of the few remaining craftsmen who made cigars by hand in 1972. He worked in his Ybor City shop from 4 a.m. into the night, turning out approximately 50 cigars an hour. *Courtesy Archives of the St. Petersburg Times*

OPPOSITE: A Shore Acres family evacuates during flooding caused by Hurricane Agnes in June 1972. *Courtesy Archives of the St. Petersburg Times*

"Mr. Nixon Should Resign or Be Impeached, October 22, 1973

"Like most people in this country, the *Times* until now has sought solutions to Watergate that did not include the extreme step of resignation or impeachment of President Nixon. But the President's unrestrained attempt to stop the independent prosecution of the Watergate crimes and his unreasonable purge of the Justice Department are so far outside the normal rules of constitutional government that the national interest now requires that Mr. Nixon resign, or if he refuses, that he be impeached."

ABOVE: Pinellas County Commissioner William D. Dockerty, followed by Republican political organizer Jack Insco, strides out of the Pinellas jail on October 21, 1975, after posting bail. Dockerty and two commission colleagues – George Brumfield and A. Oliver McEachern – went to prison following a mid 1970s political corruption investigation that was prompted by disclosures in the *St. Petersburg Times*. *Courtesy Archives of the St. Petersburg Times*

LEFT: Front page of the *St. Petersburg Times*, August 9, 1974. *Courtesy Special Collections and Archives, Nelson Poynter Memorial Library, University of South Florida St. Petersburg*

BELOW: Tampa police salute the coffin of former detective Richard Cloud, who was 33 when he was gunned down in a Mafia-style assassination on October 23, 1975. Cloud, who had been fired by the Police Department several months earlier, was investigating organized crime and allegations of police corruption at the time of his death. Seven men were eventually convicted for their role in the murder. Anthony Antone, the man who masterminded the hit, was executed in January 1984. *Courtesy Archives of the St. Petersburg Times*

ABOVE: A car with a license plate ending with an odd number hopes to slip through and get some gas during the nation's energy crisis in February 1974. *Courtesy Archives of the St. Petersburg Times*

RIGHT: Bill O'Donnell relaxes with a book and the *Times* while waiting for gas during the energy crisis in 1974. *Courtesy Archives of the St. Petersburg Times*

BELOW: The ribbon-cutting ceremony for Countryside Mall in September 1975. From left are Fred Heise, general manager; Stuart Golding, developer; Clearwater Mayor Gabe Cazares; Charles Rutenberg, chairman of U.S. Home; and E.M. Craig, a representative of Sears. The mall's opening signaled a movement of the residential area from the center of Clearwater to the north. *Courtesy Archives of the St. Petersburg Times*

"Let's Begin Rebuilding Downtown, September 19, 1975

"Every thriving city must have a heart – a gathering place, a focal point, one location that symbolizes the whole community, in short, a downtown. In St. Petersburg, our heart has been sick. The disease is complex, there is little to be gained by rehashing it.

What is important is that the fact of downtown's decline be recognized and followed by a determination to begin rebuilding it.

...The latest report deserves a different response. It says some harsh things that needed saying out of pride, if for no other reason, it should prod us into action. Let's begin."

LEFT: Front page of the *St. Petersburg Times*, April 30, 1975. *Courtesy Special Collections and Archives, Nelson Poynter Memorial Library, University of South Florida St. Petersburg*

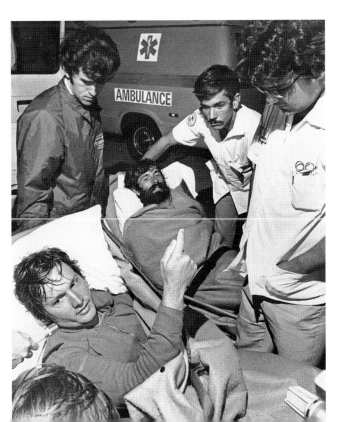

ABOVE: Krumhorn Quartet entertains Sun City Center residents during the holiday season in 1974. Musicians (from left) are Dr. John Phelps, Dr. Maurice Whitney and Dr. and Mrs. Hans Neuberger. *Courtesy Archives of the St. Petersburg Times*

TOP LEFT: Even though construction of what would become Interstate 275 began in the early 1960s in northern Hillsborough County, the route through downtown Tampa and St. Petersburg to Manatee County wouldn't be fully completed until the mid 1980s. Here work is being done on the 16th Street N overpass in St. Petersburg in December 1976. *Courtesy Archives of the St. Petersburg Times*

LEFT: Crewmen Mann Bradley and Doug O'Brien are hustled to ambulances at Albert Whitted Airport in St. Petersburg in October 1976 after being rescued from a 36-hour ordeal in the Gulf of Mexico. Their ship, the *Moomie G*, capsized, dumping them and two other shipmates into the chilly waters. They had been given up for dead until rescuers saw a light flashing in the dark. *Courtesy Archives of the St. Petersburg Times*

ABOVE: A large photo of L. Ron Hubbard, the founder of the Church of Scientology, hangs in one of the church's properties, the former Bank of Clearwater, in 1979. When the church bought the Fort Harrison Hotel, a Clearwater landmark, four years earlier, it concealed its identity for months, disclosing it only after repeated complaints from city officials and investigations by the *Times* and *Clearwater Sun*. Documents seized by the FBI later showed that Scientologists staged a phony hit-and-run accident in an attempt to smear Mayor Gabe Cazares, tried to discredit reporters and their relatives, infiltrated the *Sun* and obtained private correspondence from the *Times* and its lawyers. The *Times* won a Pulitzer Prize in 1980 for disclosures about the church's activities. Clearwater is now the international spiritual headquarters for the church, which by 2008 had 29 properties in Clearwater, most downtown. *Courtesy Archives of the St. Petersburg Times*

RIGHT: Dancers in the dress of several of their homelands (or those of their ancestors) join one another in the Sponge Exchange in Tarpon Springs during the annual International Glendi Festival, October 1977. *Courtesy Archives of the St. Petersburg Times*

ABOVE: The Swashbucklers cheer on the Tampa Bay Buccaneers during the team's first year in the National Football League in 1976. *Courtesy Archives of the St. Petersburg Times*

RIGHT: An estimated 8,000 fans turned out to welcome the Bucs home and celebrate the team's first win after going 0-26 in its first two seasons. The Bucs beat the New Orleans Saints 33-14 in the Superdome on December 11, 1977. *Courtesy Archives of the St. Petersburg Times*

BELOW: More than 7,000 race fans shows up at Sunshine Speedway's motocross course to watch the nation's top riders complete for the National 500cc title, August 1977.
Courtesy Archives of the St. Petersburg Times

ABOVE: Owner Hugh Culverhouse and Coach John McKay (waving hat) greet fans who welcomed the Bucs home after their first NFL victory. *Courtesy Archives of the St. Petersburg Times*

ABOVE: The 79-foot *Kialoa* prepares to sail under the Skyway during the Southern Ocean Racing Conference (SORC) race on January 29, 1977. The boats raced from St. Petersburg to Boca Grande and back, a distance of 138 miles. *Courtesy Archives of the St. Petersburg Times*

TOP RIGHT: Spinnakers set full, a segment of SORC fleet approaches the Sunshine Skyway on January 29, 1977. *Courtesy Archives of the St. Petersburg Times*

RIGHT: This jockey and his mount were covered with mud at the Florida Downs and Turf Club (Tampa Bay Downs) during the grand opening in 1977. *Courtesy Archives of the St. Petersburg Times*

ABOVE: Little Patty Schwartz gets a hand from firefighter Dennis Gast as she tries on his gear at Fire Station No. 1 in St. Petersburg, circa 1977. *Courtesy Archives of the St. Petersburg Times*

TOP LEFT: The Manatee County Fair begins with a ribbon cutting in Palmetto in January 1977. From left are fair president Richard B. Ernest, conquistador Jim Ryan, Miss Manatee Donna Hatcher, Charles Wooten Jr. a Hernando De Soto, and Richard Aalberg, the fair's general manager. *Courtesy Archives of the St. Petersburg Times*

LEFT: The Pier remains a popular spot for dining, sightseeing and fishing along St. Petersburg's waterfront in 1977. *Courtesy Archives of the St. Petersburg Times*

ABOVE: *Times* chairman Nelson Poynter speaks after a groundbreaking ceremony at the University of South Florida in St. Petersburg. He was instrumental in bringing the campus to the city. He died a few hours later at the age of 74 on June 15, 1978. *Courtesy Special Collections and Archives, Nelson Poynter Memorial Library, University of South Florida St. Petersburg*

BELOW: Jerry Braun and his wife, Jean, and their children Linda and Jake munch on fried chicken while passing the time leading up to a Tampa Bay Bucs game in September 1978. *Courtesy Archives of the St. Petersburg Times*

ABOVE: Front page of the *St. Petersburg Times*, June 16, 1978. *Courtesy Special Collections and Archives, Nelson Poynter Memorial Library, University of South Florida St. Petersburg*

ABOVE: Officials comb through the wreckage at High Point Elementary near Pinellas Park after a tornado reduced the school to a splintered shell in May 1978. Three children died and 60 were injured in the storm. About 125 students were having a lunch of potato turbot, green beans and banana cake in the cafeteria when the tornado hit. *Courtesy Archives of the St. Petersburg Times*

TOP RIGHT: Many fathers and mothers, hearing of the tornado, raced to the scene where there were reunions such as this one. *Courtesy Archives of the St. Petersburg Times*

RIGHT: The community comes together after the tragedy at High Point Elementary. It was a day for volunteering, from giving blood to playing with scared children at a hospital. *Courtesy Archives of the St. Petersburg Times*

ABOVE: Stewards calm eager greyhounds before a race at Derby Lane in St. Petersburg in 1979. *Courtesy Archives of the St. Petersburg Times*

LEFT: T.J. Eller is one of the fans who gets primed any Sunday the Tampa Bay Bucs are at home in 1979. During this game against the Minnesota Vikings, his bell wasn't enough to carry his team to victory. *Courtesy Archives of the St. Petersburg Times*

BELOW: Hang glider Hal Elgin stages his sixth annual Thanksgiving Hang Glider Fly-In in St. Petersburg Beach in November 1979. *Courtesy Archives of the St. Petersburg Times*

The 1980s

For a quarter century, the region's most conspicuous landmark seemed virtually indestructible. The Sunshine Skyway was so high, so strong that state road planners expected it to last well into the 21st century. But calamity came in May 1980, when a freighter knocked down part of the southbound span and 35 people died. For the next seven years, northbound and southbound motorists shared the remaining span while a new Skyway – higher, stronger, better protected – was built.

Civic boosters liked to call Tampa "America's next great city," and there were abundant signs of progress. The Hyatt Regency Hotel and City Center went up downtown near a new parking garage. After that came Harbour Island, a development on a man-made island south of downtown. A new performing arts center opened, and so did several luxury office towers.

Amid the glitter, however, a criminal shadow government was at work in Hillsborough County, at least according to federal prosecutors. County Commissioners Jerry Bowmer, Fred Anderson and Joe Kotvas went to jail for taking payoffs. More than a dozen others were charged, but most were acquitted. The county's chief judge and state attorney came under investigation, but neither was charged. In another man's trial, Gov. Bob Martinez found himself denying that he took illegal campaign contributions and gifts while running for mayor of Tampa in 1979. Afterward, he tried without success to get bombastic U.S. Attorney Robert Merkle ousted from his job.

Hillsborough was also home to the first major figure convicted in Wall Street's insider trading scandal. Paul Bilzerian was fined $1.5-million and sent to jail for 13 months for securities fraud and tax crimes. For years thereafter, his 28,363-square-foot mansion – who owned it, what it was worth – kept Bilzerian in the news.

In St. Petersburg, the last segment of Interstate 275 opened.

So did the first two buildings at a new campus for the University of South Florida St. Petersburg, followed by the Salvador Dali museum and Jannus Landing, a downtown shopping, restaurant and entertainment district. Grander plans flopped, however. Voters overwhelmingly rejected Pier Park, a proposed shopping and recreation center along the waterfront, in 1984. Three years later, the City Council hired a master planner called Bay Plaza Cos. to turn a nine-block section of downtown into a ritzy Mediterranean-style village with three upscale department stores, dozens of shops and restaurants, and parking garages. When Bay Plaza gave up in 1995, the only accomplishment was a $14-million parking garage with two floors of commercial space.

St. Petersburg spent the '90s in pursuit of a baseball team. It dismantled the 70-year-old Municipal Gas Plant tanks, displaced the large black neighborhood surrounding it, and built a domed stadium that opened in 1990. Major League Baseball was not encouraging, however, and an attempt to lure the White Sox from Chicago failed in the 11th hour. Most leaders in Tampa, which also was seeking a team, derided St. Petersburg's efforts. A *Tampa Tribune* editorial said the White Sox should pick Tampa over St. Petersburg, which the editorial compared to "a particularly pinched Albanian village."

Pasco and Hernando counties continued the growth spurts that began in the late 1950s and '60s. Pasco's population grew by almost 90,000 to 281,131 in the '80s and Hernando's more than doubled to 101,115. Two devastating freezes ended Hernando's days as a major citrus producer.

In 1987, the *Times* began a major expansion into Tampa. St. Petersburg, Clearwater and Pinellas were essentially built out, newcomers were flocking to the Hillsborough suburbs and studies suggested that central and east Pasco would grow rapidly as well. Moreover, as *Times* chairman Eugene Patterson told readers, the communities of Tampa Bay were growing together into "Florida's biggest city…the city of Tampa Bay." The expansion and the dedication of a new $12-million building in St. Petersburg capped Patterson's career at the paper. On October 31, 1988, he handed control of the company to Andrew Barnes, an executive he had brought to St. Petersburg from the *Washington Post* and groomed to succeed him.

LEFT: Redskins quarterback Joe Theismann is pursued by Howie Long of the Raiders in Super Bowl XVIII at Tampa Stadium on January 23, 1984. The Raiders won 38-9. Tampa would go on to host two more Super Bowls: New York Giants versus Buffalo in 1991 and Baltimore and New York Giants in 2001. Tampa will also host Super Bowl XLIII in February 2009. *Courtesy Archives of the St. Petersburg Times*

ABOVE: Salvage workers manage to raise the Coast Guard buoy tender *Blackthorn* from the bottom of Tampa Bay. On January 28, 1980, the *Blackthorn* sank after colliding with the tanker *Capricorn* near the Sunshine Skyway bridge, killing 23 crew members. It was the Coast Guard's worst peacetime disaster. *Courtesy Archives of the St. Petersburg Times*

TOP RIGHT: The *Blackthorn* was severely damaged after it collided with the tanker.
Courtesy Archives of the St. Petersburg Times

RIGHT: Twenty-seven *Blackthorn* crew members were able to escape the sinking ship. A memorial inscribed with the names of the 23 crew members who perished now stands two miles north of the site of the accident. *Courtesy Archives of the St. Petersburg Times*

LEFT: Front page of the *St. Petersburg Times,* May 10, 1980. In a blinding rainstorm on May 9, 1980, the phosphate freighter *Summit Venture* collided with the Sunshine Skyway, collapsing the structure and sending six cars, a pickup and a Greyhound bus 150 feet into Tampa Bay. Thirty-six people were aboard the vehicles; 35 died. One car, above, Paul Hornbuckle's 1976 Buick Skylark, came to a stop just 14 inches from the edge. At 7:34 a.m., the ship hit a support column of the southbound span, bottom. A quarter-mile chunk of the bridge, far left, plunged into the bay. *Courtesy Archives of the St. Petersburg Times*

ABOVE: More than 200 people gathered outside the 460-room, all-wood Belleview Biltmore Hotel for ceremonies honoring the old Victorian building, which was entered on the National Register of Historic Places, Clearwater, March 1980. *Courtesy Archives of the St. Petersburg Times*

BELOW: Tampa Bay Rowdies fans cheer on their team as they beat the Detroit Express 3-2 for first place in the American Conference's Eastern Division, August 1980. Fans of the Rowdies were called Fannies. The most famous Fannies were the notorious North End Zone Gang (also known as the Ozone, the Yellow Card Section, The Mooners and the Village Idiots). The gang of college-age fans were known for their wild antics, including throwing dead mullet dressed in mini uniforms of rival Fort Lauderdale Strikers onto the field. *Courtesy Archives of the St. Petersburg Times*

ABOVE: Johnny Cash and June Carter Cash perform a benefit concert for the police benevolent funds of Port Richey and New Port Richey, December 1980. For years, the famous couple owned a second home overlooking the Pithlachascotee River in Port Richey. *Courtesy Archives of the St. Petersburg Times*

BELOW: With the 1979 Tampa Bay Buccaneers making the playoffs, fans read the paper to pass the time in the predawn hours while waiting to buy tickets for the conference championship game against the Los Angeles Rams on January 8, 1980. The Bucs lost 9-0. *Courtesy Archives of the St. Petersburg Times*

ABOVE: Paul Eppling with his sculpture *Water Stork*, created with old car bumpers, Largo, January 1980. Eppling fashioned his sculptures from metal that he found. He combined automobile bumpers with industrial scraps and welded on electrical conduit or any other appropriate metal until he was satisfied with the result. *Courtesy Archives of the St. Petersburg Times*

TOP RIGHT: When Nelson Poynter died in 1978, control of the *Times* and the school that owns it passed to Eugene Patterson. A highly decorated veteran of World War II, Patterson had been a Pulitzer Prize winner at the *Atlanta Constitution*, managing editor of the *Washington Post* and teacher at Duke University. Under his guidance, the paper's staff exposed corruption from the state Capitol to the county courthouse. *Courtesy Archives of the St. Petersburg Times*

RIGHT: After singing *Happy Birthday* to 15-year-old Lucifer, Susan Daly tells him to open wide…then tosses the carrot cake with 15 carrot candles into the ready jaws of the hippopotamus, Homosassa Springs, January 1981. In one gulp, it was gone. *Courtesy Archives of the St. Petersburg Times*

They're Coming Home..., January 21, 1981

"**The long and sorry ordeal** of the 52 Americans kidnapped by the government of Iran finally has ended. The prudence of the U.S. government saved the lives of the hostages, won their freedom and protected the national honor.

The flights to freedom came almost exactly at the end of President Carter's term. Thus, Carter left office on the happy note of successfully completing complex and difficult negotiations for the goal he most wanted to accomplish."

ABOVE: At the Chasco Fiesta Festival, the legend of Queen Chasco and King Pithla is retold and acted out by residents in the New Port Richey area. In 1981, Robert Shevlin, (left) Gina Diglio, Frank Berardi (child) and Alan Gardner act out the legend. *Courtesy Archives of the St. Petersburg Times*

TOP RIGHT: Republican presidential candidate Ronald Reagan shakes hands with the crowd at St. Petersburg-Clearwater International Airport during a campaign stop on March 10, 1980.
Courtesy Archives of the St. Petersburg Times

RIGHT: Mellisa Davis and her bassett hound Lady won Funniest Dressed at the Chasco Fiesta Dog Show in New Port Richey, 1981. *Courtesy Archives of the St. Petersburg Times*

OPPOSITE LEFT: Front page of the *St. Petersburg Times*, January 21, 1981.
Courtesy Special Collections and Archives, Nelson Poynter Memorial Library, University of South Florida St. Petersburg

OPPOSITE RIGHT: Front page of the *St. Petersburg Times*, January 14, 1982.
Courtesy Special Collections and Archives, Nelson Poynter Memorial Library, University of South Florida St. Petersburg

America Prays for the President, March 31, 1981

"Stunned. Anguished. Outraged. Shamed.

Words fail to convey the enormity of America's agony.

Caught once again in the awful maelstrom of emotions, a shaken, prayerful nation today gives thanks for the survival of President Reagan.

Solemnly, we join America's hopeful vigil for the President's complete, speedy recovery from the assassination attempt Monday and mourn the tragic shooting of James Brady, the presidential press secretary."

ABOVE: Seven members of the "Largo 8" are recognized at a meeting of the Largo Chamber of Commerce. The eight men, all over 60, were convicted of gambling in 1982 after authorities raided their penny ante poker game at their mobile home park. The arrests became national news. Radio talk shows were flooded with calls from people outraged at the charges. CBS News sent a reporter to cover the trial, in which the Largo 8 were convicted, given one month of probation and fined $75 apiece. People sent them money. One anonymous donor gave them $150 each. A Clearwater restaurant saluted them with a free meal. And a casino flew the men and their wives to Atlantic City for three days of fun and legal gambling. *Courtesy Archives of the St. Petersburg*

RIGHT: Bill Noto carries world champion gopher tortoise racer Tommy Butler at the San Antonio Rattlesnake Festival and International Championship Gopher Races in 1981. Butler's fleet-footed entry Ozzy captured victory on what has been billed as "the world's slowest track." *Courtesy Archives of the St. Petersburg Times*

FAR RIGHT: Hundreds of spectators stand outside of St. Nicholas Greek Orthodox Cathedral in Tarpon Springs on January 6, 1981, as Archbishop Iakovos, center, steps outside of the cathedral just before the start of the annual Epiphany parade. *Courtesy Archives of the St. Petersburg Times*

ABOVE: Gary Anderson (43) lunges across goal line for the Tampa Bay Bandits in May 1984. The USFL team went on to beat the New Orleans Breakers 31-20 to put them in a commanding position to win a spot in the USFL playoffs. *Courtesy Archives of the St. Petersburg Times*

ABOVE: Florida state Rep. Douglas "Tim" Jamerson and state Sen. Jeanne Malchon appear at a community forum Jamerson sponsored in 1982 in St. Petersburg. Jamerson was the first African-American legislator elected from Pinellas County. He went on to become the state commissioner of education and secretary of the state's Department of Labor and Employment Security. He died in April 2001.
Courtesy Archives of the St. Petersburg Times

RIGHT: St. Petersburg had the attention of the art world in 1982 when the doors opened to the Salvador Dali Museum, which houses a $35-million collection of the artist's works. The collection, which includes 93 oil paintings, numerous watercolors and drawings and a 2,500-volume library on Dali and Surrealism, was donated by A. Reynolds and Eleanor Morse of Cleveland. *Courtesy Archives of the St. Petersburg Times*

BELOW: A fire that officials say was deliberately set destroyed a row of buildings in downtown St. Petersburg in October 1982. Officials estimated the damage at $1.2-million. The block included the Tarpon Bar, shown here as firefighters fought the blaze.
Courtesy Archives of the St. Petersburg Times

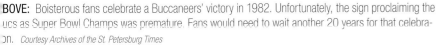

ABOVE: Boisterous fans celebrate a Buccaneers' victory in 1982. Unfortunately, the sign proclaiming the Bucs as Super Bowl Champs was premature. Fans would need to wait another 20 years for that celebration. *Courtesy Archives of the St. Petersburg Times*

TOP RIGHT: Clearwater's Amy Benz (left) and golf celebrity Lee Trevino were partners at the JC Penney Golf Classic at Bardmoor Country Club, December 1983. *Courtesy Archives of the St. Petersburg Times*

RIGHT: Derek Bell pitches during a Southern Regional Little League game in Gulfport in 1981. Bell helped Tampa's Belmont Heights Little League team reach the finals of the World Series in 1980 and '81, losing to Taiwan both times. He went on to an 11-year major-league career with the Blue Jays, Padres, Astros, Mets and Pirates. Other Belmont Heights Little League graduates include Gary Sheffield, Carl Everett and Dwight "Doc" Gooden. *Courtesy Archive of the St. Petersburg Times*

OPPOSITE: Director Ron Howard is shown filming the lunch counter scene at Woolworth's in Northeast Shopping Center for the movie *Cocoon*, St. Petersburg, 1984. *Courtesy Archives of the St. Petersburg Times*

ABOVE: Director Ron Howard discusses a scene with actors Hume Cronyn and Don Ameche outside the Snell Arcade, St. Petersburg, 1984. *Courtesy Archives of the St. Petersburg Times*

TOP LEFT: More than 3,000 people turned out under the sun in downtown St. Petersburg in 1983 for the "Sunshine Jamboree" at Jannus Landing. *Courtesy Archives of the St. Petersburg Times*

LEFT: Renee Bolan, 19 months of Dade City gives her gopher a push during the gopher race at the Rattlesnake Festival and International Championship Gopher Races in San Antonio, 1984. Gone are the days of Craig Miller and "Whizzer," who holds the record for the 50-foot long course. Miller used to train his turtle on a special track in his back yard in Bradenton and in 1976 jockeyed Whizzer to win in 24.2 seconds.
Courtesy Archives of the St. Petersburg Times

Our Second Century, July 26, 1984

"Newspaper work, as it must be, is obsessed with the future. The idea of tomorrow's newspaper, and those that will follow, becomes a companion for all who work at shaping it. That is one reason this 100th anniversary year has been a special one for members of the staff of the *St. Petersburg Times*. While working on tomorrow's newspapers, we had the pleasure of exploring the rich chapters of our past.

...Our wish is that, when we and our community mark the end of our second century, it will be said that by reporting the news and searching for its true meanings the *St. Petersburg Times* helped light the way as brightly in its second 100 years as it did in its first."

ABOVE: Doug Williams joined the Tampa Bay Buccaneers out of Grambling State in 1978. He led the Bucs to three playoff appearances and one NFC title game. After winning the NFC Central Division in 1981, Williams left in 1982 after a contract dispute.
Courtesy Archives of the St. Petersburg Times

TOP RIGHT: Crowds enjoy a beautiful day on the beach in Pass-a-Grille, December 1984. The Don CeSar Beach Resort Hotel is in the background. *Courtesy Archives of the St. Petersburg Times*

RIGHT: Children, from left, Kristin Kent, Ingrid Pfaffman, Nathan Pfaffman and Jeffery Kent watch as hot-air balloons take off during centennial celebrations in Ybor City, January 1986.
Courtesy Archives of the St. Petersburg Times

"Catastrophe at the Cape,
January 29, 1986

"A deep sense of loss overwhelms the American people. No American astronaut ever before had been killed in flight. Now, we mourn the deaths of six astronauts and a schoolteacher.

The nation's response to the explosion of the space shuttle *Challenger* was the same as those who witnessed the tragedy at Cape Canaveral – stunned disbelief, horror, sadness.

There was nothing to forebode the catastrophe we were about to see. Like so many times before, the gleaming ship rose spectacularly off the launch pad and was climbing gloriously toward the heavens. Little more than a minute later, a gigantic fireball raged in the sky over the Atlantic off the Kennedy Space Center.

....Today, we also should remember the thrill, the challenge and the glory of reaching for the heavens – a tribute to the gallant space explorers the nation has lost."

ABOVE: Suspended Pasco County Sheriff John Short and his son Michah wave to motorists during Short's campaign for re-election in 1984. A series of stories that began in 1983 investigated relationships between Short and several of his employees, including John Moorman, a millionaire whom Short made a deputy. Short and Moorman were indicted on charges of unlawful compensation but the charges against Moorman were dropped and Short was acquitted. In 1985 the *St. Petersburg Times* won a Pulitzer Prize for the series. *Courtesy Archives of the St. Petersburg Times*

TOP LEFT: Three nights of rioting erupted in Tampa in February 1987 after the death of a mentally handicapped black man, Melvin Eugene Hair, who died after police used a carotid neck-hold on him. During the riots, police sealed off a 12-block area. At the end of three nights, 200 to 400 people had burned and looted a grocery store and torched trash bins and a station wagon. Seven were injured; 14 arrested. *Courtesy Archives of the St. Petersburg Times*

LEFT: In 1979, Beneficial Corp. bought an island near Tampa's port from Seaboard Coast Line and built Harbour Island. The development's first phase opened in 1985 and included a 300-room hotel, an office building and retail center. *Courtesy Archives of the St. Petersburg Times*

185

"Happy Centennial!, June 8, 1988

"**June 8, 1888 was a** happy day in the town that came to be St. Petersburg. The steam locomotive Mattie, pouring out black smoke and soot, pulled the first train into the Ninth Street station from Oakland, the town near Orlando that was headquarters of the Orange Belt Railway. .....From that small beginning, led by Peter A. Demens and Gen. John C. Williams, a great community has risen. A full program of events to celebrate the city's centennial began in January and will continue through December."

ABOVE: After five years of construction, the new $240-million Sunshine Skyway bridge was dedicated with a daylong ceremony that stretched into the night on February 7, 1987. The evening was capped by a fireworks display as the lights on the new bridge's support cables were turned on. The bridge was opened for traffic on April 30, 1987. *Courtesy Archives of the St. Petersburg Times*

LEFT: A wind-chill factor of 37 degrees failed to deter more than 20,000 people from turning out on January 11, 1987, for the Dedication Run of the new Sunshine Skyway bridge. Buses at the top of the bridge shuttled runners and walkers back to the land sides. *Courtesy Archives of the St. Petersburg Times*

OPPOSITE: For years, Civil War buffs have carried out battle re-enactments as part of the Annual Brooksville Raid Festival, bringing to life a glimpse of a war-torn past. On July 7, 1864, Union forces landed at Bayport in Hernando County and marched toward Brooksville. Their objective: a supposed Confederate base funneling supplies to troops in Georgia and Virginia. The Confederates attempted to block the Union advance about six miles from town, but could do little more than harass the northern troops. On July 9, the Union troops swept through the Confederate camp and into Brooksville, routing the outnumbered Confederates and putting the torch to several buildings. *Courtesy Archives of the St. Petersburg Times*

ABOVE: Vice President George Bush arrives in Tampa during a campaign swing on July 24, 1988. At far left is his son, Jeb Bush, who would later become governor of Florida. To the right of George Bush is then-Gov. Bob Martinez of Tampa. *Courtesy Archives of the St. Petersburg Times*

RIGHT: Racing in the St. Petersburg area dates back to 1985. The Trans-Am Series races circled St. Petersburg's waterfront until 1990 near the Bayfront Center, drawing noise complaints from many business owners and residents. Here, Scott Schubot's crew checks out his car during a Camel GTP Light practice in 1989.
Courtesy Archives of the St. Petersburg Times

FAR RIGHT: About 35 newspaper and yearbook students from 16th Street Middle School in St. Petersburg were treated to a tour of the construction site of the Florida Suncoast Dome in January 1988. The stadium was completed in 1990. It was called the ThunderDome while the Tampa Bay Lightning were tenants, and it was renamed Tropicana Field in October 1996. *Courtesy Archives of the St. Petersburg Times*

189

The 1990s

The Tampa Bay area's long, contentious quest for baseball finally ended in 1995, when Major League Baseball awarded a team to St. Petersburg. The decade also saw the arrival of a hockey team, the Lightning, and a successful campaign to finance a new stadium for the Buccaneers. That kept the football team in Tampa.

Although Bay Plaza's makeover of downtown St. Petersburg fizzled out, there was a resurgence after all. It was sparked by the reopening of the Vinoy hotel in 1992 and the arrival of the Florida International Museum three years later. The museum's first exhibits drew big crowds, which over time spawned new restaurants, shops and nightclubs.

Tampa got two big projects in the '90s. The city borrowed $156-million to build a downtown convention center, but it took another nine years to get a large convention hotel nearby. The Florida Aquarium opened to big crowds and positive reviews, but it soon was struggling with financial problems.

Racial issues percolated and sometimes flared. Tampa's annual Gasparilla parade was canceled in 1991 when Ye Mystic Krewe, the all-male, all-white group that sponsors it, refused to admit black members. (The parade resumed the next year after the group relented.) St. Petersburg's white police chief, Curt Curtsinger, was fired in 1992 by the acting city manager, who was black, for alleged racial insensitivity and poor management skills. The ouster of the popular chief further polarized a city electorate already divided over downtown revitalization projects and the taxes to support them. Curtsinger sued the city, settled for $585,000, then narrowly lost a bitter campaign for mayor in 1993.

Three years later, a young black man was shot and killed by a white St. Petersburg police officer in a confrontation during a traffic stop. It touched off rioting that flared again three weeks later when a grand jury cleared the officer. The incidents

prompted changes at City Hall, which increased spending in black neighborhoods, and the Police Department, which got its first black police chief – Goliath Davis – in 1997. Tampa's first black chief, Bennie Holder, was appointed four years earlier.

In 1993, 12-year-old Jennifer Odom got off her school bus in rural Pasco County and disappeared. Her body was found six days later; her murder is still unsolved. In 1997, 5-month-old Sabrina Aisenberg disappeared from her home in a Tampa suburb. She is still missing.

Lisa McPherson, a 36-year-old Scientologist, was involved in a minor traffic accident in Clearwater in 1995. But when she removed her clothes, police took her to a hospital for a psychiatric evaluation. Representatives of the Church of Scientology soon whisked her away to the church's headquarters. After 17 days there, McPherson died. As the case played out over nine years, the state attorney filed criminal charges, then dropped them. McPherson's family filed a wrongful death suit, then abruptly settled out of court, under terms that remained confidential.

Traffic sometimes seemed to overwhelm the region's roads and bridges. But there were improvements. A second span of the Howard Frankland Bridge opened in 1991. The old span was widened and in 1993 there were four lanes going in each direction. That same year saw completion of the Bayside Bridge, which linked south Pinellas to Clearwater across Old Tampa Bay. Then came the Veterans Expressway, a 15-mile toll road into northwest Hillsborough from the Courtney Campbell Parkway.

In the 1990s, the *Times* won three Pulitzer Prizes. Each one was welcome news for the staff, which earlier in the decade wondered if Nelson Poynter's model for the paper would survive. Some *Times* stock that Poynter reluctantly sold his sister in 1947 had passed to her daughters upon her death. The daughters, in turn, sold the stock to investors led by billionaire Robert Bass. For almost two years, Bass and the *Times* – now led by Andrew Barnes – sparred over ownership of the paper in the courts of law and public opinion. It ended in August 1990, when the Bass group agreed to sell its stock to the *Times* for $56-million.

TOP RIGHT: Flames rocket hundreds of feet into the air and heavy black smoke spews from the barge *Ocean 255* in Tampa Bay on August 10, 1993, after it and another barge collided with the *Balsa 37*, a 400-foot freighter. *Ocean 255* carried jet fuel, oil and gasoline. No one was injured but about 330,000 gallons of oil and another 32,000 gallons of jet fuel spilled from the two barges into the bay and fouled beaches and waterways all along Pinellas County. *Courtesy Archives of the St. Petersburg Times – Fred Victorin*

ABOVE: Giant topiaries and lots of pastel colors replaced the normal look of the Carpenters Run subdivision in Pasco County when the movie *Edward Scissorhands* was filmed there in the spring of 1990. *Courtesy Archives of the St. Petersburg Times – Jack Rowland*

TOP: A daunting challenge awaited Andrew Barnes when he took over the *Times* in 1988. An investor group led by Texas billionaire Robert Bass had acquired *Times* stock from Nelson Poynter's nieces, and it wanted control of the newspaper. After two tense years, the *Times* bought out the Bass group for $56-million – finally securing the independence of the paper. On his 65th birthday in 2004, Barnes stepped aside for a new chairman, Paul C. Tash.
Courtesy Archives of the St. Petersburg Times

RIGHT: Mayor Sandy Freedman, who became Tampa's first female mayor in 1986, announces on June 25, 1993, that Bennie Holder will be Tampa's first black police chief. Holder inherited a department that continued to suffer from distrust created during the 1980s when several young black men were killed or beaten during run-ins with police officers. *Courtesy Archives of the St. Petersburg Times – Victor Junco*

ABOVE: Just after a midday rain, cars pass through the stream that was 58th Street S, north of 22nd Avenue in St. Petersburg on August 13, 1997. *Courtesy Archives of the St. Petersburg Times – Ricardo Ferro*

LEFT: A coating of ice drips from an orange at Brandon Farms after a freeze settled over the fields of Hillsborough County in January 1996. *Courtesy Archives of the St. Petersburg Times – Jim Stem*

BOTTOM LEFT: "It's better than a high school reunion," says Lynn Colombo as she practices for the 50th reunion celebration at Weeki Wachee Springs on October 4, 1997. Colombo worked as a mermaid at the Hernando County attraction from 1973 to 1986. *Courtesy Archives of the St. Petersburg Times – Toni L. Sandys*

BELOW: The North and the South square off again at the 15th annual Brooksville Raid Festival in January 1995 at Sand Hill Scout Reservation in Spring Hill. The festival re-enacts an 1864 Civil War skirmish. *Courtesy Archives of the St. Petersburg Times – Ollie Stonerook*

ABOVE: Suncoast Waterworks team member Lorna Fountain (front) leads members of the synchronized swimming team during a practice on February 5, 1995, in Highland Pool in Largo. Established in 1985, Suncoast WaterWorks is considered one of Florida's premier teams. *Courtesy Archives of the St. Petersburg Times – Scott Keeler*

TOP RIGHT: Members of the Zephyrhills skydiving team City Soup pull into a formation as they freefall from 13,500 feet over Skydive City in Pasco County on December 29, 1995. Eighty skydivers in four teams competed over two days to see which team could do the most midair formations. *Courtesy Archives of the St. Petersburg Times – Tony Hathaway*

BOTTOM RIGHT: An adult sandhill crane spreads its wings and pecks at Steve Nesbitt, a biologist with the Game and Fresh Water Fish Commission, on March 3, 1995. Game officers were trying to remove two crane eggs from a nest in East Lake where cranes had died in traffic over the years. The brown, speckled eggs were taken to a breeding farm in Northeast Florida. *Courtesy Archives of the St. Petersburg Times – Joan Kadel Fenton*

BELOW: State biologist Monica Ross approaches a male manatee in the Crystal River in Citrus County on June 20, 1997. The manatee is closer to the camera than the swimmer, and so appears somewhat larger than he is. Nevertheless, at about 8 feet in length, and weighing 600 to 800 pounds, he is no lightweight. In fact, said Ross, "I think he was about the fattest wild manatee I've ever seen." The marks on the animal's flippers are not propeller scars. They are fat folds. *Courtesy Archives of the St. Petersburg Times – Bill Serne*

Terrorism Hits Home, April 20, 1995

"**Terrorism is terrorism, whether it** is perpetrated by organized cults of religious fanatics or by lone assailants driven by personal demons. So whatever the motivations of the murderer or murderers responsible for the bombing of a federal office building in Oklahoma City, the crime was a particularly despicable act of terrorism.

....Any remaining illusion that Americans are somehow less vulnerable to terrorism, and therefore less responsible for helping to lead international anti-terrorism efforts, was demolished this week.

Our hearts go out to those in Oklahoma City whose lives have been shattered by an act of terrorism that defies human comprehension.

Our minds also turn to our own loved ones, and the terrible realization that their own well-being is not nearly as snugly insulated from the world's horrors as we would like to pretend."

LEFT: Heavy thunderstorms moved through the Tampa Bay area over a weekend in August 1994, producing heavy rain and spectacular lightning displays, including this strike on the Sunshine Skyway. *Courtesy Archives of the St. Petersburg Times – Eric Parsons*

An Amicable Parting, September 29, 1995

"**Bay Plaza has gone away.** Not that it was ever really here in the first place. Bay Plaza began with the promise of a massive, upscale shopping mall in the middle of downtown St. Petersburg, but the plan kept shifting and shrinking, until nothing was left but the faint hope of a movie theater. With Thursday's announcement that it is finally pulling out entirely after more than eight years of bluff and bluster, Bay Plaza leaves behind little more than a 6-block hole in the middle of an otherwise thriving downtown."

ABOVE: Vice President Al Gore, right, and Republican challenger Jack Kemp face off at a debate at the Mahaffey Theater in St. Petersburg on October 9, 1996. Produced by the Commission on Presidential Debates, the event was brought to St. Petersburg by a host committee including the *St. Petersburg Times*, the city of St. Petersburg, the University of South Florida and the St. Petersburg-Clearwater Convention & Visitors Bureau. *Courtesy Archives of the St. Petersburg Times – Ricardo Ferro*

LEFT: At least 8,000 people jammed historic Pass-a-Grille to see the rock group the Spin Doctors on July 4, 1996. Others never made it. Gridlock stretched miles back to Interstate 275, forcing police to close the two-lane road leading into Pass-a-Grille to vehicular traffic. The city of St. Pete Beach had been expecting 2,500 people. *Courtesy Archives of the St. Petersburg Times – Ricardo Ferro*

"Picking up the Pieces, October 26, 1996

"The people of St. Petersburg and surrounding communities cannot afford to ignore the racial divisions that helped turn a police shooting into an ugly explosion of arson, rock-throwing and other violence Thursday night. Such criminal behavior can never be condoned, and those responsible for it should be aggressively prosecuted. However, the anger and despair that emanate from St. Petersburg's most blighted neighborhoods are entirely understandable. People from all walks of the community must find constructive ways to address the social and economic issues that are at the heart of that anger."

ABOVE: Led by Chief Darrel Stephens (in dark green shirt and blue jeans), police officers and residents clash at 16th Street and 18th Avenue S in St. Petersburg on Oct. 24, 1996, after a white officer killed a young black man during a traffic stop. Two nights of arson and gunfire followed the fatal shooting of TyRon Lewis, 18, who police said was shot and killed when his car lurched toward the officer. *Courtesy Archives of the St. Petersburg Times – Brian Baer*

BELOW: Hank Earl Carr, center, was an ex-convict who kept a handcuff key on him and was wanted in three states. On May 19, 1998, Carr was being arrested in the shooting death of his girlfriend's 4-year-old son when he escaped. He killed two Tampa police detectives, Randy Bell, left, and Rick Childers, far right, and led authorities on a wild chase through three counties. Along the way he murdered Florida Highway Patrol Trooper James "Brad" Crooks before killing himself during a standoff at a gas station in Hernando County. *Courtesy Archives of the St. Petersburg Times – Ken Helle*

ABOVE: President Bill Clinton spoke of racial harmony at St. Paul A.M.E. Church in downtown Tampa on November 3, 1996, and met with St. Petersburg leaders in the wake of the Oct. 24 riot. "You know after the events of the last week, when we are divided, we defeat ourselves," Clinton told the congregation. *Courtesy Archives of the St. Petersburg Times – Jim Stem*

ABOVE: Before the $332-million Veterans Expressway opened in October 1994, more than 1,000 runners took part in 5- and 10-kilometer races on the highway that stretches nearly 15 miles from the Courtney Campbell Parkway to N Dale Mabry Highway in Lutz. *Courtesy Archives of the St. Petersburg Times – Kathleen Cabble*

BELOW: Spectators at Air Fest '96 at MacDill Air Force Base in Tampa wait in line on April 13, 1996, to get inside a KC-10 Extender which is used for carrying payloads and refueling. The two-day event features military hardware and flying machines old and new. It generally draws crowds of more than 600,000. *Courtesy Archives of the St. Petersburg Times – Victor Junco*

ABOVE: Gen. Norman Schwarzkopf displays the velvet-lined box holding a medal designating him Honorary Knight Commander of the Bath while his wife, Brenda, looks on. During a two-hour visit to Tampa on May 20, 1991, Queen Elizabeth II of England, left, knighted the general for commanding all allied forces during Operation Desert Storm in Iraq. *Courtesy Archives of the St. Petersburg Times – Maurice Rivenbark*

The Beginning of a Beautiful Relationship, March 31, 1998

"....Consider Tampa Bay's long, obsessive pursuit of a franchise to call our own.

For at least 20 years, this community looked to baseball as its ticket to the major leagues, or at least to national respectability.

....The important thing is, Tampa Bay finally has its team. The Devil Rays' first real game is today. We're in the big leagues, in the same division with the New York Yankees, the Boston Red Sox, the Baltimore Orioles and the Toronto Blue Jays. That's rich company – rich in tradition, and rich in money.

....Tampa Bay wants baseball. But baseball needs Tampa Bay. The realization of our satisfying reversal of fortune with the longtime object of our desire adds a touch of spice to this day of community celebration."

ABOVE: The grounds crew spreads 350 tons of Tennessee dirt in the infield at Tropicana Field in St. Petersburg. *Courtesy Archives of the St. Petersburg Times – Jonathan Newton*

TOP LEFT: Front page of the *St. Petersburg Times*, April 1, 1998. *Courtesy Archives of the St. Petersburg Times*

LEFT: Stan Musial plays *Take Me Out to the Ballgame* on his harmonica on March 31, 1998, during the first ever Devil Rays game. It was played at Tropicana Field. *Courtesy Archives of the St. Petersburg Times – Cherie Diez*

OPPOSITE: History in the making as Belinda Womack and a 75-voice choir sing the National Anthem for the opening games with 45,369 fans packing the stands. *Courtesy Archives of the St. Petersburg Times – Jonathan Newton*

201

A New Century

As west-central Florida entered the 21st century, it had grown together into one of the most dynamic metropolitan regions in the country. The population of Pinellas had soared to 921,495; Hillsborough to 998,948; Pasco, 344,765; and Hernando, 130,802. The Tampa Bay area was now the biggest media market in what political strategists called a "battleground state." No wonder so many national candidates visited so often.

When the 42-mile Suncoast Parkway opened in 2001, it extended the Veterans Expressway through Pasco and Hernando to a point just south of Citrus County. It also hastened population growth in both counties and effectively pushed the metropolitan area farther north. Some government leaders said it was time to explore mass transit.

It was a region that always seemed to be in the national news. There was the debate over the feeding tube of Terri Schiavo, the custody battle over a child known as "Baby Sam" and the abduction and murder of 9-year-old Jessica Lunsford. The son of celebrity wrestler Hulk Hogan went to jail after he wrapped a sports car around a tree and left his passenger disabled for life. And Largo City Manager Steve Stanton disclosed that he intended to change his name to Susan and live as a woman. He was fired.

The Tampa Bay Buccaneers won the Super Bowl in 2003 and the Tampa Bay Lightning won the Stanley Cup in 2004. Four years later, the Tampa Bay Rays became the second team in Major League history to make the playoffs the year after posting the worst record in baseball.

In both Pinellas and Hillsborough, decades-old desegregation plans ended and majority black schools started to reappear. Most black parents seemed to favor a return to nearby schools, but there was continuing concern over an achievement gap between white and black students.

Clearwater voters soundly rejected a $300-million redevelopment of the downtown waterfront bluff, but there were new signs of economic life in other urban centers. The Centro Ybor complex, which featured theaters, restaurants and shops, opened in Tampa. So did BayWalk, a similar venture in St. Petersburg. Tampa got International Plaza, a high-end regional mall. St. Petersburg residents voted to preserve the Albert Whitted Airport and watched high-rise condominiums go up downtown.

For a time, the Tampa Bay area's housing market sizzled, much as it had in the Florida boom of 1920-26. Home prices soared, and frenzied speculators bought houses and condominiums just to flip them to new buyers at a profit. In late 2006, however, the overheated market started to cool. Florida suddenly found itself in a deep, lengthy recession.

One hundred and twenty-five years after it started as a country weekly in Dunedin, the *Times* was the state's largest paper with an average daily circulation of 318,306 and average Sunday circulation of 432,779. The paper that once embraced Jim Crow now had two black members on its board of directors. It remained privately owned and independent, just as Nelson Poynter planned.

The *Times* also faced formidable challenges – the worst newspaper economy since the Great Depression and fundamental changes in readers' needs and tastes. For many years, the *Times* could concentrate on one product, the paper. Now, it also offered electronic delivery of the news – via the Web – and a free daily tabloid for younger readers in a hurry. Paul C. Tash was chairman now, and resolutely optimistic that both the *Times* and Tampa Bay had great days ahead. In a memo in 2008, he called on the staff "to recommit ourselves to the difficult but vital work of adapting the *Times* to changing consumer tastes and challenging economic times. By bringing our creative energy and best efforts to this task, we serve the best interests of our customers, our company and ourselves. Now, let's get on with it."

LEFT: There was a clash of priorities on March 10, 2007, as two weddings at the Rheba Sutton White Chapel ran smack into a daylong bicycle race through downtown Palm Harbor. The Gearlink Cup caused delays and upset two brides and their guests, but both weddings eventually went ahead as planned.
Courtesy Archives of the St. Petersburg Times – Ted McLaren

EXTRA!
St. Petersburg Times

RECOUNT

Gore concedes to Bush then retracts as national
cliffhanger turns on final tally of Florida votes

GORE 249
BUSH 246

At 5 a.m., the campaigns called it a night. Bush led Gore in Florida by less than 600 votes. Gore appeared headed for a win in the national popular vote. A full day of recounting and bickering lies ahead. **Full coverage inside.**

ABOVE: Florida Gov. Jeb Bush, left, introduces his brother and Republican presidential candidate George W. Bush at a Florida Victory 2000 rally in Tampa on September 22, 2000.
Courtesy Archives of the St. Petersburg Times – Chris Schneider

TOP LEFT: Democratic presidential candidate Al Gore, right, and running mate Sen. Joseph Lieberman leave the Florida Bakery in Tampa about 5:30 a.m. during a last-minute campaign stop on Election Day, November 7, 2000. The results of the contested election would not be known for several weeks. *Courtesy Archives of the St. Petersburg Times – Ken Helle*

TOP RIGHT: Front page of the *St. Petersburg Times*, November 8, 2000.
Courtesy Archives of the St. Petersburg Times

RIGHT: Front page of the *St. Petersburg Times*, December 14, 2000.
Courtesy Archives of the St. Petersburg Times

SPECIAL SECTION INSIDE
COMMEMORATIVE 12-PAGE RECAP OF THE LAST 36 DAYS

IT'S HISTORY

St. Petersburg Times
Florida's Best Newspaper

WEATHER: High 82, low 65; 20% chance of rain. More, 8B

THURSDAY, December 14, 2000   25¢

PRESIDENT BUSH

5-week ordeal ends with pledges of unity

By MARY JACOBY and DAVID KARP
Times Staff Writers

"We will stand together behind our new president."
–VICE PRESIDENT AL GORE

Gore pledges he'll work to unify nation

■ The vice president says he "strongly" disagrees with the Supreme Court decision but will accept it.

The 10 reasons
Here are the many factors, large and small, that propelled George W. Bush to a 537-vote victory in Florida, giving him the presidency. **7A**

Still Supreme?
Baffling, jarring, even contradictory. With their ruling, the justices may have diminished the Supreme Court as an institution. **3A**

Yeah, show us
Democrats in Congress say it's one thing for the new president to preach working together– he has to prove he means it. **4A**

Tainted votes
Florida elections officials find tainted votes as they match the number of signatures on precinct books to the ballots actually cast. **1B**

Senators wait
Uncertain about what the candidates would say, the state Senate holds off a vote on a resolution to name electors for George W. Bush. **6B**

By BILL ADAIR
Times Staff Writer

WASHINGTON – In a poignant end to an extraordinary election, Vice President Al Gore on Wednesday conceded the presidency to Texas Gov. George W. Bush and vowed to help his Republican rival unite the nation.

"This is America," Gore said. "Just as we fight hard when the stakes are high, we close ranks and come together when the contest is done."

In a deeply personal speech that came, incredibly, five weeks after Election Day, Gore offered the nation something it had desperately wanted: closure.

"Let there be no doubt, while I strongly disagree with the court's decision, I accept it. I accept the finality of this outcome which will be ratified next Monday in the Electoral College. And tonight, for the sake of our unity as a people and the strength of our democracy, I offer my concession."

Gore spoke from an ornate room at the Eisenhower Executive Office Building adjacent to the White House. His running mate Joe Lieberman and their families stood silently beside him during the seven-minute speech. At one point, Lieberman clutched Tipper Gore's hand.

Millions of Americans watched the nationally televised speech to see if Gore would seek to bridge the partisan chasm that has wid-

Please see **GORE 6A**

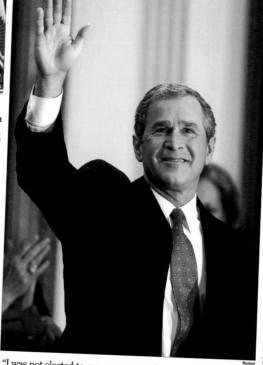

"I was not elected to serve one party, but to serve one nation."
–PRESIDENT-ELECT GEORGE W. BUSH

Battle changes a changing Florida

By TIM NICKENS
Times Political Editor

Times files–SCOTT KEELER
Gov. Jeb Bush has bridges to rebuild with black voters; 93 percent opposed his brother.

ANALYSIS

The image appears familiar, yet the changes are unmistakable.

Florida will deliver its 25 electoral votes to George W. Bush just as it was expected to do a year ago. There still is a popular Republican governor, who now happens to be the president-elect's younger brother. And Republicans remain in firm control of the Legislature.

But Florida looks decidedly different in the wake of the historic battle over the presidency. Deep scars now crease its sunny face of theme parks and beaches. The state is sharply divided along political and racial lines. Republicans are esca-

lating their attacks on the Florida Supreme Court. Democrats are portraying the Legislature as an arm of the Bush campaign, and the credibility of the state's elections system is in shambles.

The battle has affected individuals as well as institutions.

Gov. Jeb Bush, whose approval ratings have dropped slightly but remain high, no longer appears untouchable if he runs for re-election in two years. Secretary of State Katherine Harris, who became internationally recognizable for her role in the post-election fight, has watched her political fortunes plummet. State Supreme Court Justice Harry Lee Anstead faces an

Please see **NICKENS 4A**

AUSTIN, Texas
Before a cheering crowd of friends, family and Texas state legislators, George W. Bush accepted the presidency Wednesday evening, saying it is "time to find common ground and build consensus."

His 15-minute speech from the Texas House of Representatives chamber in the state Capitol capped the end of a bizarre five-week period of legal battles over who had won the state of Florida and its crucial 25 electoral votes. The battles ended Tuesday evening when the U.S. Supreme Court issued a decision that ended the Florida recount.

"Our country has been through a long and trying period, with the outcome of the presidential election not finalized for longer than any of us could have ever imagined," Bush said. "So I understand how difficult this moment must be for Vice President Gore and his family."

It was a muted speech, coming five weeks after Bush aborted his plans to claim victory in the early hours of Nov. 8 when Gore, noting that the Florida results were still unsettled, called the governor in Austin to retract a concession.

At 8:52 a.m. Wednesday, Gore finally called back to concede for good. Bush said he and his former rival agreed to meet early next week in Washington, "to do our best to heal our country after this hard fought contest."

And healing will certainly be needed. Not only does Bush become the first president since 1888 to lose the nationwide popular vote but prevail in the Electoral College, but he also faces questions about his legitimacy. He will lead a congress where Republicans are barely in control.

Bush tried to begin that healing in his speech. "I was not elected to serve one party, but to serve one nation," he said.

Bush chose to address the nation from the Democratic-controlled Texas House, where he was introduced by Speaker James E. "Pete" Laney, a Democrat and close friend.

"Here, in a place where Democrats have the majority, Republicans and Democrats have worked together to do what is right for the people we represent," Bush said. "We had spirited disagreements, and in the end, we found constructive consensus. It is an experience I will always carry with me, and an example I will always follow."

He added: "The spirit of cooperation I have seen in this hall is what is needed in Washington. It is the challenge of our moment."

His brother, Florida Gov. Jeb Bush, issued a statement shortly before the televised address.

Please see **BUSH 8A**

INDEX

Jumble 7D
Ann/Abby 7D
Astrology 7D
Bridge 7D
Business 1-8E
Classified F
Comics 8D
Crossword 7D
Editorials 18A
Entertainment 2B

Letters 19A
Lottery 2A
Movies 5D
Parimutuels 5D
Sports 1-8C
Television 7D

Vol. 117 - No. 143
2 sections

LEFT: Front page of the *St. Petersburg Times*, September 12, 2001.
Courtesy Archives of the St. Petersburg Times

ABOVE: Sgt. 1st Class Paul Smith, a 33-year-old who grew up in Tampa, was shot and killed in Iraq in 2003 while holding off advancing Iraqi forces as his men made it to safety. *Courtesy Matthew Hartley*

BELOW: As his sister Jessica, his mother, Birgit, and President George W. Bush applaud during a White House ceremony on April 4, 2005, David Smith, 11, accepts the Medal of Honor awarded to his late father. *Courtesy Archives of the St. Petersburg Times – Brendan Fitterer*

RIGHT: Front page of the *St. Petersburg Times*, January 27, 2003. *Courtesy Archives of the St. Petersburg Times*

TOP RIGHT: Bucs head coach Jon Gruden leads a sideline celebration after Keenan McCardell's touchdown in the closing minutes of the second quarter. Tampa Bay dominated the Oakland Raiders in the first half and overcame some missteps in the second to win its first Super Bowl on January 26, 2003. *Courtesy Archives of the St. Petersburg Times – Jim Damaske*

BOTTOM RIGHT: The Tampa Bay Lightning became the NHL champions on June 8, 2004, by holding off the Calgary Flames to win Game 7 2-1. That summer, the Stanley Cup journeyed the world as Lightning players took 24-hour turns with it. Here, Nolan Pratt, the last player to get the Cup, strips down to his Calvin Klein boxers and makes for water at Clearwater Beach.
Courtesy Archives of the St. Petersburg Times – Dirk Shadd

OPPOSITE: Front page of the *St. Petersburg Times*, June 9, 2004. *Courtesy Archives of the St. Petersburg Times*

St. Petersburg Times
Florida's Best Newspaper

MONDAY, January 27, 2003

SUPER BOWL XXXVII

TAMPA BAY 48 — OAKLAND 21

CHAMPS

Coach Jon Gruden embraces defensive tackle Warren Sapp after the Bucs routed the Oakland Raiders. The team returns to Tampa to share the glory with the hometown fans tonight.

OUTSTANDING VICTORY

Coach Jon Gruden and the nation's No. 1 defense lead the Bucs to their first NFL title, with a convincing victory over his old team. 1X

WATCHING THE CLOCK

The streets were quiet and stores were deserted as ordinary life took a back seat to waiting for the outcome of the game. 2A

TAKING IT TO THE STREETS

But as the game ended, fans poured out of their homes and bars looking to share the historic moment for the community. 3A

MUSICAL INTERLUDE

From Celine Dion and the Dixie Chicks to Shania Twain, No Doubt and Sting, this Super Bowl rocked and twanged. 6A-7A

HAIL THE HEROES

Stadium gates open at 7 tonight for the Bucs' return about 9 p.m. A victory parade is planned for 3:30 p.m. Tuesday in Tampa. 3A

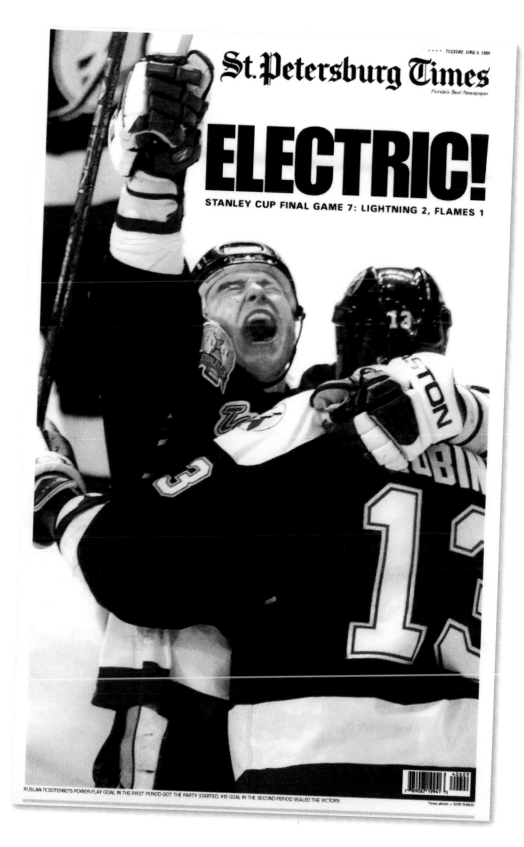

St.Petersburg Times
Florida's Best Newspaper

TUESDAY, JUNE 8, 2004

ELECTRIC!

STANLEY CUP FINAL GAME 7: LIGHTNING 2, FLAMES 1

RUSLAN FEDOTENKO'S POWER-PLAY GOAL IN THE FIRST PERIOD GOT THE PARTY STARTED. HIS GOAL IN THE SECOND PERIOD SEALED THE VICTORY.

Times photo — DIRK SHADD

A Cleansing Postscript, December 14, 2000

"**President-elect George W. Bush and** Al Gore took the first steps toward moving the country beyond a nasty campaign that dragged on for five extra weeks....Gore conceded with grace, humor and a lack of rancor, admonishing his supporters that 'our disappointment must be overcome by our love of country.' Still the second-guessing for Gore must be agonizing. No losing presidential candidate had ever won the national popular vote by such a large margin – or lost the decisive state by such a small one."

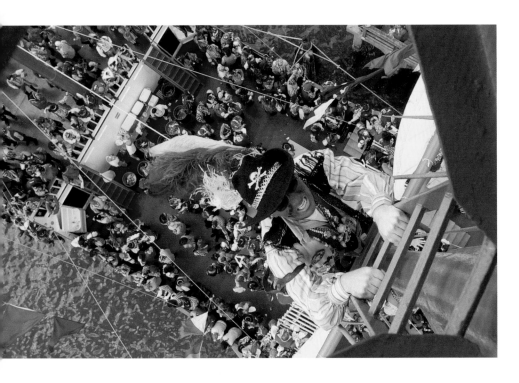

ABOVE: Pirate Blake Casper climbs the rigging of the José Gasparilla on February 2, 2002, where he will have a crow's-nest view of the invasion and parade in Tampa. *Courtesy Archives of the St. Petersburg Times – John Pendygraft*

RIGHT: Lucio Torres loads flats of freshly picked strawberries on the back of a truck that will carry them a short distance to a roadside stand at Brandon Farms in Valrico in February 2000.
Courtesy Archives of the St. Petersburg Times – Jamie Francis

BELOW: A young alligator peers through a patch of duckweed north of Riverview Heights in Citrus County on a dreary November afternoon in 2005. *Courtesy Archives of the St. Petersburg Times – Max Bittle*

ABOVE: Jason Paris, 27, of Kentucky, tapes up for his first ride of the night on April 5, 2002, as Tim Edge, 23, of Mississippi watches as the gates are set for the first round of competition at the 2002 Odessa Rodeo. *Courtesy Archives of the St. Petersburg Times – Brendan Fitterer*

TOP LEFT: Jodi Smith, 17, of Holiday spends part of the first day of the Florida State Fair upside down on the Tango on February 6, 2003. *Courtesy Archives of the St. Petersburg Times – John Pendygraft*

LEFT: Athletes begin the St. Anthony's Triathlon by entering Tampa Bay for the .93-mile swim on April 27, 2003. *Courtesy Archives of the St. Petersburg Times – James Borchuck*

ABOVE: Rachael Laky, 9, browses art pieces at the Mainsail 2005 "Young at Art" tent April 7, 2005, at Vinoy Park in St. Petersburg. Behind her are paintings from students at Gibbs High School. The tent displayed about 700 creations, many for sale, from students of all ages in Pinellas County's public and private schools. *Courtesy Archives of the St. Petersburg Times – Lara Cerri*

BELOW: Harry Liquerman, 77, and his girlfriend, Ivy Brown, 71, both of St. Petersburg, enjoy a tea dance at the historic Coliseum in St. Petersburg on December 19, 2007. The couple had met two years earlier at a tea dance. *Courtesy Archives of the St. Petersburg Times – Scott Keeler*

ABOVE: A Hoosier like Paul and Nelson Poynter, Paul C. Tash started at the *Times* as a summer intern in 1975 and became chairman 29 years later. "I feel a particularly keen obligation to Nelson Poynter, that little guy in a bow tie who gave away his life's work because he believed in an idea," said Tash.
Courtesy Archives of the St. Petersburg Times

BELOW: Helio Castroneves, with Team Penske, smiles while being mobbed by race fans as he rides his scooter from pit row in April 2008 after a practice session during the fourth annual Grand Prix of St. Petersburg. *Courtesy Archives of the St. Petersburg Times – Dirk Shadd*

ABOVE: Christine Marriott of Seminole stands with her dog, Kiska, outside Hospice House Woodside in the early hours of March 25, 2005, where dozens of people stood vigil for Terri Schiavo. Schiavo, 41, was the subject of a national debate over the removal of her feeding tube. Doctors said she was in a persistent vegetative state, and her husband, Michael Schiavo, decided to have the feeding tube removed. Her parents wanted her kept alive and went to court. After a lengthy court fight, the feeding tube was removed. She died 13 days later. *Courtesy Archives of the St. Petersburg Times – Carrie Pratt*

BELOW: A soldier salutes the coffin of Pfc. Marc Delgado during Delgado's funeral in Brandon on December 6, 2005. Delgado, 21, of Riverview, was killed in Iraq on Thanksgiving when an explosive device flipped his vehicle into a canal. *Courtesy Archives of the St. Petersburg Times – Brian Cassella*

ABOVE: A riderless horse with boots turned backward leads the coffin of Sgt. Ron Harrison, 55, a Hillsborough sheriff's deputy of more than 27 years. Harrison was shot to death in the early hours of August 15, 2007, not long after leaving a drunken driver checkpoint. Authorities say 24-year-old Michael Allen Phillips ambushed the deputy. Phillips later died in an exchange of gunfire with a SWAT team. *Courtesy Archives of the St. Petersburg Times – Brian Cassella*

ABOVE: Brian Afaayo, 9, center, sings on January 15, 2008, in Tampa with the Watoto Children's Choir of Uganda to kick off the University of South Florida's celebration of Dr. Martin Luther King Jr. The choir is part of Watoto, a Christian organization that cares for orphans and strives to raise them as the country's next generation of leaders. Watoto means "children" in Swahili, and the group's choir has toured internationally since 1994 to bring attention to Africa's wars and HIV-AIDS crisis. *Courtesy Archives of the St. Petersburg Times – Kathleen Flynn*

BELOW: From left, front, Auneshia Whitson, 13, D'Ahjene Murray, 5, Indya Gibson, 4, and Darta Murray Jr., 8, watch the bands and floats on January 21, 2008, along Dr. Martin Luther King Jr. Street during the Drum Major for Justice National Parade. Bands from across the nation come to march in the annual parade in St. Petersburg. *Courtesy Archives of the St. Petersburg Times – Scott Keeler*

The Role of Bloggers,
February 26, 2005

"**The proliferation of Internet Web** logs – so-called 'blogs' – has unsettled mainstream news organizations that have become a prime target for bloggers. On the whole, it's probably a healthy development. The news media have a credibility problem and bloggers, for all their excesses, have shown they have a role to play in holding mainstream journalists accountable.

....Mainstream journalists have nothing to fear from bloggers if they remain true to fundamental standards of accuracy and fairness. They must remain cautious before passing along information from blogs or reacting to their charges, while continuing to learn from a form of mass media that is evolving before our eyes. Blogging, if practiced responsibly, could boost old media's credibility by making it more accountable to the public."

ABOVE: Tarpon Springs sponge boat owner and diver Muhip Goktepe cleans wool sponges on the back of his friend's boat, the *St. Phillip*, on March 26, 2004, at the historic Tarpon Springs Sponge Docks. *Courtesy Archives of the St. Petersburg Times – Scott Keeler*

LEFT: Joe Duff, co-founder and team leader of Operation Migration, is followed by six whooping cranes as his ultralight flies over the U.S. Fish and Wildlife Service office in Crystal River on December 3, 2001, near the end of the endangered birds' journey. The trip, which covered more than 1,200 miles, began Oct. 17 in the Necedah National Wildlife Refuge, about 90 miles northwest of Madison, Wis. *Courtesy Archives of the St. Petersburg Times – Steve Hasel*

ABOVE: Achilleas Houllis, 18, of Tarpon Springs emerges from the chilly waters of Spring Bayou with the cross on January 6, 2002, at the annual Epiphany celebration in Tarpon Springs. Whoever retrieves the cross is said to be blessed for the following year.
Courtesy Archives of the St. Petersburg Times – Scott Keeler

LEFT: Barbara Kelly, 81, left, samples the little fruit with a big taste at the 10th annual Kumquat Festival in Dade City on January 27, 2007. "I like the sweet kumquats, but not the sour ones!"
Courtesy Archives of the St. Petersburg Times – Julia Kumari Drapkin

FAR LEFT: Pilot John Mohr, of St. Paul, Minnesota, flies over downtown St. Petersburg and Demens Landing on October 19, 2007, in his 1943 Stearman biplane in preparation for the annual St. Petersburg AirFest at Albert Whitted Airport.
Courtesy Archives of the St. Petersburg Times – Martha Rial

ABOVE: In July 2008, Florida Gov. Charlie Crist became engaged to his girlfriend of nine months, Carole Rome, who is president of her family's 100-year-old Halloween costume business. Crist proposed to Rome in his Bayfront Tower condominium in St. Petersburg. "God bless her, she said yes," he said.
Courtesy Archives of the St. Petersburg Times – Scott Keeler

BELOW: Sen. Hillary Rodham Clinton mingles with the audience after speaking at the Wyndham Westshore hotel in Tampa on February 25, 2006, as part of a fundraising reception for the Florida Democratic Party.
Courtesy Archives of the St. Petersburg Times – William Dunkley

ABOVE: Republican presidential candidate Sen. John McCain greets supporters at the Tampa Convention Center during a rally on September 16, 2008. *Courtesy Archives of the St. Petersburg Times – Scott Keeler*

BELOW: Democratic presidential candidate Sen. Barack Obama greets the crowd at a rally in the St. Pete Times Forum on May 21, 2008, in Tampa. The bay area was a frequent stop for candidates from both parties. *Courtesy Archives of the St. Petersburg Times – Chris Zuppa*

ABOVE: J.P. Howell, Gabe Gross and Eric Hinske charge onto the field after the Tampa Bay Rays beat the Minnesota Twins 7-2 on September 20, 2008, to clinch the Rays' first ever trip to the playoffs. Many of the players, and quite a few fans, adopted Mohawk haircuts for the end of the season. *Courtesy Archives of the St. Petersburg Times – Edmund Fountain*

LEFT: Pitcher Scott Kazmir, center, and his teammates celebrate after their win over the Twins. *Courtesy Archives of the St. Petersburg Times – Cherie Diez*

FAR TOP LEFT: The front page of the September 21, 2008, *St. Petersburg Times* echoes the Rays improbable accomplishment. The team became only the second team in major-league history to reach the playoffs after having the worst record in the majors, joining the 1991 Atlanta Braves, and the third team to do so after 10 consecutive losing seasons, joining the 1914 Boston Braves and the 2006 Tigers. *Courtesy Archives of the St. Petersburg*

FAR BOTTOM LEFT: Manager Joe Maddon and catcher Dioner Navarro embrace after reaching the playoffs. The Rays clinched the AL east division and defeated the Chicago White Sox in the American League Divisional Series. *Courtesy Archives of the St. Petersburg Times – James Borchuck*

OPPOSITE: Rays catcher Dioner Navarro blocks the plate and tags Phillies centerfielder Shane Victorino to complete a double play in Game 2 of the World Series on October 22, 2008, at Tropicana Field in St. Petersburg. The Rays won the game, but lost the series to Philadelphia 4-1. *Courtesy Archives of the St. Petersburg Times – Dirk Shadd*

2008 AMERICAN LEAGUE CHAMPION TAMPA BAY RAYS

Monday, October 20, 2008

St. Petersburg Times

HISTORY IN THE MAKING

HELLO, WORLD!

The Rays complete a 3-1 victory over the Red Sox to win the AL title and advance to their first World Series.

BRIAN CASSELLA | Times

World Series Game 1: vs. Philadelphia, Wednesday at Tropicana Field | 8 p.m. | Ch. 13

ABOVE: The October 20, 2008, front page of the *St. Petersburg Times* announces the Tampa Bay Rays' first trip to the World Series after the team defeated the defending champion Boston Red Sox. In the series, the Philadelphia Phillies proved to be too tough for the young Rays. *Courtesy St. Petersburg Times*

RIGHT: The Rays clinch their first pennant in Game 7 of the American League Championship Series on October 19, 2008, when Akinori Iwamura fields Jed Lowrie's grounder and tags second base to end the game 3-1 against the Boston Red Sox. *Courtesy Archives of the St. Petersburg Times – Dirk Shadd*

Index